WALKS AROUND MALMESBURY
& NORTH WILTSHIRE

Judy Jones

Blue Tree Books

First published in 2008 by
Blue Tree Books, 28 Back Hill,
Malmesbury, Wiltshire,
SN16 9BT
United Kingdom

A catalogue record for this book is available from the British Library.

ISBN 978-0-9557682-0-0

Printed on recycled paper and bound in Great Britain by
CPI Antony Rowe, Chippenham, Wiltshire

Contents

Contents

Acknowledgements

Grateful thanks to the route testers whose helpful input is reflected in the final text: Sue Alexander, Bill and Julie Cavendish, Doreen Chandler, Steve and Hilary Cox, Ginny Parfitt, Glyn and Linda Davies, Mike Elam, Vanessa Fortnam-King, Marion Farrelly and Paul Mewton, Carolyn and Ian Kennedy, Anna Palmer, Trish Pollard, and Lesley Saunders. I am indebted to Mary Ray Smith for the title illustration showing the geographical area featured in the book, the walk titles and numbers. Thanks also to Sue Austin for proof reading the text and formatting my computer files. I also thank the landowners, public rights of way officers and others who work to maintain the vast network of footpaths and bridleways around Malmesbury and North Wiltshire.

The mapping used to create the route sketch maps featured in this book is reproduced by permission of Ordnance Survey on behalf of HMSO © Crown Copyright 2007. All rights reserved. Ordnance Survey Licence number 100047744.

Foreword

The long search for a lost dog provided the inspiration for this book. Over the summer of 2001, I spent four wretched weeks trying to find my newly-acquired collie Fly after she went missing in 600 acres of woodland at Westonbirt Arboretum, near Tetbury. All sorts of people rallied round and joined the hunt after I put up posters and appealed for help through the columns of the Standard local newspaper. The Citizens' Advice Bureau ladies at Tetbury, who seemed to know every landowner personally for miles around, scanned the farms listed in the Yellow Pages and suggested which ones might be worth contacting.

Regular sightings, tips and offers of help soon flowed in – phone calls, notes stuffed through my letter box and people flagging me down in the street. Friends, family and fellow dog walkers locally helped me look for Fly; an ex-soldier put his considerable tracking skills at my disposal during one sweep of woodland near Easton Grey, and other pals came up from London to join the hunt. I heard of householders putting food out for the dog just in case she was passing through, horse riders keeping an eye out on early morning hacks over King's Heath. Much to my relief, finding Fly appeared to have turned into a collective effort that gathered momentum with every passing week. Eventually, the dog and I were reunited in a barn near Norton, about five miles south west of our home in Malmesbury.

Searching for the dog had been a humbling experience, a turning-point in my life. It opened my eyes to the glorious landscape around Malmesbury, north Wiltshire and its borders with Gloucestershire: beautiful countryside, villages and remote hamlets, steeped in fascinating history – all on my doorstep.

Perhaps, I wondered, this was an area that people tended to drive through, or glimpse from a railway carriage – as I had done before acquiring my dog – rather than explore on foot. I soon resolved to explore the area's public rights of way more systematically, devise some circular routes and then to publish a book of these walks so that others can enjoy them too. The featured routes are mostly in north Wiltshire, on the border with Gloucestershire or just north of the county boundary. Sprawling south from the heart of the Cotswolds to the northern outcrops of the Wiltshire Downs are quiet stretches of farming country, parkland, streams and rivers – the infant Thames, the Wiltshire Avon (Sherston and Tetbury branches), the Vale of Dauntsey, green lanes and ancient landscapes. The many public rights of way that criss-cross it, permissive paths and minor lanes provide great opportunities to explore and enjoy what the area has to offer. By walking these long-established routes, we can help preserve them for future generations. Some of them may otherwise simply disappear – through neglect and over-growth, cultivation or development. It's our choice – we use them or we may lose them.

About this Guide

The 25 walks vary in length, difficulty and landscape. They are designed to appeal to a broad range of walkers, from beginners and weekend strollers to the more ambitious, and range in length from around 3 miles to 8 miles. Each walk is given a star-rating to indicate the level of physical challenge it presents:

*	Easy
**	Moderate
***	More challenging

Points of historical, cultural and architectural interest are highlighted along the way, as are some great pubs, whose phone numbers are given as they arise in the text. All timings and distances stated are approximate, and if anything, over-estimated. Although not essential, you may wish to take the relevant OS map with you to get the most out of the walk. Most of the 25 routes described are within the area covered by OS Explorer Map: Stroud, Tetbury and Malmesbury (No. 168). The rest are within the Chippenham and Bradford-on-Avon OS Explorer Map area (No. 156), Marlborough (No. 157) or Cirencester & Swindon (169).

Walking safely and responsibly

The better you prepare for walking, and anticipate potential problems, the more you will get out of the experience. Ensure that you are properly clothed and equipped for the great outdoors, and aware of your legal responsibilities, as well as your rights.

Only you can decide what you are prepared to lug around with you or wear. You might want to consider taking:

Backpack
Mobile phone
Water
Map and plastic map holder
Binoculars/camera
Small notebook/pen or mini-tape recorder
Waterproof jacket/trousers
Proper walking boots, with ankle support, (or good
    quality, comfortable wellies) and thick socks
Snack – fruit and/or chocolate bar
Money
Secateurs

You may also want to pack some skin protection/sun block and a wide-brimmed hat, depending on conditions.

Walking safely and responsibly

Follow the Countryside Code

* Keep to the public rights of way and permissive paths
* Leave gates and property as you find them
* Protect wildlife, and take litter home
* Keep dogs under close control, and pick up after them
* Be considerate of others

On occasions, you will walk along roads without pavements. Unless you see a good reason not to, remember to face the oncoming traffic when walking along roads, so that you and any drivers approaching you can see each other.

Encounters with livestock

If you ignore cattle, sheep or horses quietly grazing or dozing in a field and give them a wide berth, they will tend to ignore you in turn. Avoid eye contact with them, and don't talk or shout at them. Just walk quietly past them.

Dogs

If you have a dog with you, keep it under control at all times, and I would advise putting it on a lead whenever near livestock. You know your dog – landowners don't. They may shoot dogs they suspect of worrying their livestock. Why take the risk?

Footpath problems?

If you come across obstacles on a public right of way, you may wish to report these to the relevant highways authority. The Ramblers' website www.ramblers.org.uk provides a wealth of useful information and advice on walking and the law, and guidance on reporting problems to the public rights of way team. For the purposes of continuing your walk, you are entitled to find an alternative way around an obstruction on a right of way, if you are unable to remove it.

Public transport

Five of the walks described start and finish at the Market Cross in Malmesbury – Lea, Corston, Little Somerford, Malmesbury Circular Walk and Brokenborough. The Long Newnton and Westonbirt walks start and finish in Tetbury. For details of bus services operating in the area, ask at Tourist Information Centres, or phone Traveline public transport information on 0870 608 2608. Railway stations serving the area covered by the routes in this book are at Kemble, Chippenham, and Swindon.

Parking in Malmesbury:

Malmesbury lies off the A429 Chippenham to Cirencester road, five miles north of Junction 17 of the M4. The long stay car park is at the old station yard, off Gloucester Road, Malmesbury. Here's how you get there.

Coming from the direction of Chippenham and the M4:

Travelling north on the A429 go straight on at the round-about just past Malmesbury's new health centre and stay on the by-pass over the second roundabout by the water tower and a garage. Take the next turning left along Filands, and the next left after that towards the town centre. At the double mini-roundabout at the bottom of the hill, near a super-market, turn left to the pay-and-display long stay car park.

Coming from the direction of Cirencester and the M5:

Travelling south on the A429 from Cirencester, pass a garden centre on your left as you approach Malmesbury, go all the way round the roundabout by the water tower and back the way you came. Take the first turning left along Filands – opposite the garden centre – and the next left. Continue to the double mini-roundabout near a supermarket and turn left there to reach the pay-and-display long stay car park.

From this car park head towards the Abbey and turn right over the river along Mill Lane. Walk up the Abbey steps. Brass plates on the steps feature some of the key events in the town's history.

Follow the path between Abbey House Gardens (left) and the Cloister Gardens (right) to emerge by the Market Cross.

To visit the Malmesbury Tourist Information Office (tel. 01666-823748) go left here along Oxford Street, then first right into Market Lane – the office is then on your left in the Town Hall.

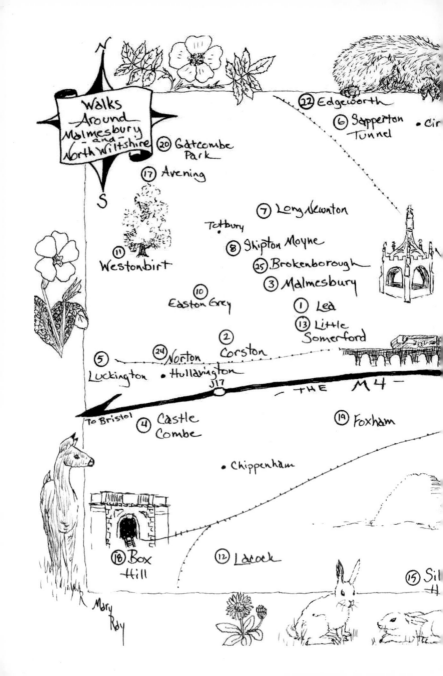

ster

⑨ Cerney Wick

Ashton Keynes

.Cricklade

Brinkworth

J16   To Swindon

Wootton
Bassett

㉑ Barbury
Castle

⑭ Avebury

The Walks

1. Lea
2. Corston
3. Malmesbury Circular Walk
4. Castle Combe
5. Luckington
6. Sapperton Tunnel
7. Long Newnton
8. Shipton Moyne
9. Cerney Wick
10. Easton Grey
11. Westonbirt
12. Lacock
13. Little Somerford
14. Avebury
15. Silbury Hill
16. Ashton Keynes
17. Avening
18. Box Hill
19. Foxham
20. Gatcombe Park
21. Barbury Castle
22. Edgeworth
23. Brinkworth
24. Norton and Hullavington
25. Brokenborough

1. LEA

Distance:	3½ miles
Time:	1¾ hours
Pub:	Rose & Crown, Lea
Map:	OS Explorer 168: Stroud, Tetbury & Malmesbury
Star-rating:	* Easy

A short walk over farmland from Malmesbury to the village of Lea via Milbourne and back over Cowbridge Weir. The Rose and Crown at Lea has a pleasant good-sized garden next to the churchyard and plenty of room inside.

Route:

From the Market Cross, Malmesbury take the lane running alongside the Whole Hog and the footpath next to the entrance to Abbey House. Go down the Abbey steps over the river bridge and straight on to reach the entrance to the **Conygre Mead (A)** nature reserve on your right. Follow the river path, from which you can glimpse through the fence part of **Abbey House Gardens (B)**, soon to meet a road junction.

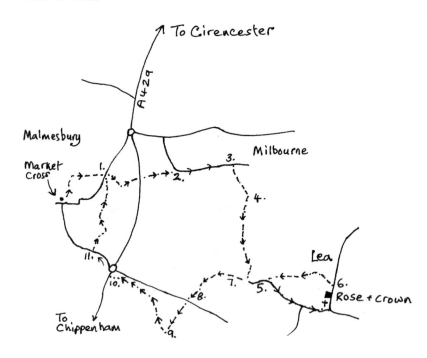

1. Turn left and almost immediately right up to Blicks Hill. You can either walk along the lane or take the footpath left through trees which runs alongside it. Cross the main road (A429) with care and go straight on through a wooden gate to walk along a lane with hedges on each side.

2. On reaching a road junction, turn right (in effect, you are continuing in the same direction) and pass a red

telephone box. Use the grass verge on the right where necessary.

3. After crossing Monks Park, take the next turning right onto a narrow lane, passing some new houses on your left. The lane soon becomes a track that leads to a large field.

4. The right of way goes diagonally right over the top of the field, but many people walk along the field edge on your right, and then turn left at the bottom corner near a metal gate. Follow the bottom edge of the field up to a stile on your right, just before a track leading to a farmhouse. Go over the stile and down the hill, bearing slightly left, towards a wooden gate near the river and a narrow lane. Once through the gate turn right onto the lane to pass Crab Mill.

5. Keep going to the end of Crab Mill Lane, turn left and then go straight on across the entrance to Pembroke Green. Follow the road as it bends left around St Giles Church. You soon reach the Rose & Crown pub (tel. 01666-824344) on your left. Continue in the same direction for about 150 yards.

6. Take the next turning left into Rushcroft Close. Go over a stile at the end of a path into a field. Bear diagonally right across the field to pass through a gate, and then go straight down the hill, keeping a hedge on your left, to meet a brook. Turn left through a gateway and then turn right towards a pair of stiles that lead you back to the lower end of Crab Mill Lane. Turn right onto the lane and, as it bends right up towards farm buildings, pass through the wooden gate (on your left) that you came through earlier.

View towards Malmesbury from hillside east of Lea

Birds on the brook near Crab Mill

7. Keeping the brook on your left, proceed along the lower edge of the field to a stile into another field. Aim for a gap in the old railway embankment ahead, once part of the **Malmesbury branch line (C),** and continue through it to a bridge over the Avon at Cowbridge Weir.

8. Follow the drive to the main road, passing the site of **Cowbridge House (D)** on your right. Cross the main

road (B4042) and pick up the footpath opposite via a stile into a field. Follow the river along the bottom edge of the field past some World War II defences then up to the top corner.

9. Turn sharp right and follow the top field edge to reach a stile into the next field. Cross this and bear diagonally left up the hill, passing a small fenced area of young trees on your left, to pass over a stile at the brow of the hill. Follow the path downhill, aiming to the right of the new health and care home complex ahead. Pass through a wide wooden gate set in the fence ahead of you into the next field. Go diagonally across the field and go over a stile in the corner. Go straight on keeping a boundary on your right over one last stile onto a track leading to a main road (A429).

10. Cross the road and bear right along the pavement down through Burton Hill and Parliament Row to reach the Town Bridge, Malmesbury. Turn left onto the foot-bridge just before reaching the road bridge, then turn right through the Memorial Gates. (On reaching the pavement, note the plaque on each gate depicting the old borough seal of Malmesbury and, on the opposite side of the road, at the junction with St John Street, a medieval hospital that later became almshouses). Turn left a few paces to a bend in the road.

11. Cross the road and continue ahead into St John Street. Go over the narrow road bridge (Goose Bridge) and keep going alongside the bowls club. Take the footpath left running alongside the far edge of the bowls club, so that you pass behind the score board. Stay on the path through two fields to reach Holloway Bridge. Cross the road, with care, and pick up the river path opposite. Follow the river path back through Conygre Mead, then retrace your steps back to the Market Cross.

Snowfall on Goose Bridge and Back Hill

Notes:

A: **Conygre Mead** is a Local Nature Reserve, providing habitats for hundreds of species of flora and fauna. The mead is owned by the Malmesbury River Valleys Trust, established in 1992, and maintained by volunteers as a place for wildlife and quiet recreation. Visit www.watervole.net/mrvt for more information.

B: Ian and Barbara Pollard, also known as the Naked Gardeners, have transformed the five-acre **Abbey House Gardens** into a riot of spring, summer and autumn colour – and an international tourist attraction. The gardens are open to the public from March to October. Visit www.abbeyhousegardens.co.uk for more information about opening times and special events.

C: **The Malmesbury branch line** operated passenger rail services from Dauntsey (on the London to Bristol main line) between 1877 and 1933 and from Little Somerford between 1933 and 1951. Freight continued to be transported along this GWR branch railway until its final closure in 1962. The station site is now occupied by Malmesbury's long stay car park and light industrial units. The history of the line is told in Mike Fenton's *The Malmesbury Branch*.

D: **Cowbridge House**, demolished in 2007 to make way for a new housing development, is thought to date back to the late 1700s. Built for members of the Brooke family of Brooke Bond Tea fame, it was later the home of Baldemiro de Bertodano, who in 1902 co-founded the St Aldhelm's Freemasons' Lodge in Malmesbury. Bob Browning's book *Ecko's of Cowbridge* tells the story of the house and the "war factory" that developed RADAR on the site.

2. CORSTON

Distance:	$6\frac{1}{2}$ miles
Time:	$3\frac{1}{2}$ hours
Pub:	Radnor Arms, Corston
Map:	OS Explorer 168: Stroud, Tetbury & Malmesbury
Star-rating:	** Moderate

Spectacular views of Malmesbury open up as you cross high farmland south west of the town en route to Corston, and its charming pond. You pass the north eastern edge of King's Heath, held by the commoners of Malmesbury for more than 1,000 years. Mainly level – you may have to climb over a gate or two.

Route:

From the Market Cross, Malmesbury, head down the High Street until you meet the Town Bridge over the Avon. Just before the bridge turn right through the Memorial Gates, and then left over the footbridge. Turn right along the pavement, go through Parliament Row, then right into Barley Close. Turn left following the left hand pavement and pass through the alleyway at the end of it to emerge onto Arches Lane.

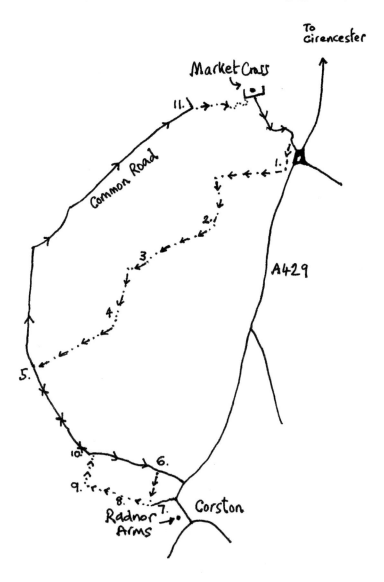

1. Turn right down Arches Lane, passing the entrance to Orchard Court, and follow the lane up to a junction of tracks near a farmhouse. Follow the lane as it bends left. When it bends left again, go through (or climb over) the middle gate of three gates you see on your right to enter a field.

2. Keeping a hedge on your left, walk uphill and follow this field edge as the land becomes more level all the way to the top left corner just beyond a large oak tree in the boundary hedge.

3. Go through a gateway and straight on at a junction of bridleways. Turn left after about 100 yards (there's a waymark on a telegraph pole), to either go over the stile, or the gate next to it if the stile is overgrown, and walk down the field aiming for a gate near the bottom right corner.

4. Pass through a walker's gap to the right of a wide gate in the field corner and turn left. Go through (or climb over) two gates separated by a wooden footbridge over a ditch and turn sharp right across the corner of a field shortly to pass through a gap in the hedge. Bear left across the next field and walk through a gateway into the next. Go straight across this towards a stile in front of a telegraph pole. Once over the stile, continue in the same direction towards a pair of stiles. Continue in the

same direction over another stile, and then one more to reach Common Road.

5. Turn left onto the road and keep going for about a mile. On your right you see **King's Heath (A)** stretching into the distance.

6. After passing three bungalows on the outskirts of Corston turn right onto a bridleway, soon to see the **Corston village pond (B)** on your left.

Corston Quarry and Pond Local Nature Reserve

7. At the end of the track, you have a choice: a) to visit the Radnor Arms (tel. 01666-823389), turn left onto Mill Lane and follow this to a junction with the A429 Chippenham-Cirencester road. Turn right along the pavement. The Radnor Arms is about 100 yards on your right. Retrace your steps back to this road junction and continue up Mill Lane. b) If not visiting the pub, turn right off the bridleway onto Mill Lane.

8. At the top of Mill Lane pass West Park House and continue through a gateway into West Park where you will see a wood away to your left.

9. Pass a line of trees. Immediately after a private drive on the right, go through a wooden gate on your right and follow the path over a stile into a field. Keep the hedge on your right as you pass to the other side of the field to exit via a stile onto Common Road.

10. Turn left to join Common Road past King's Heath again all the way to the junction with the Foxley Road.

11. Turn right and walk along the pavement until you meet a farm track coming downhill on your right. Cross the road and walk a few yards along the farm track to meet a stile on your left. Go over the stile here and follow the path through the water meadows. Take the stone footbridge over the stream on your left and follow the

View towards Malmesbury from the water meadows

stone-flagged path past the weir and another footbridge back into Malmesbury. Go across the entrance to a housing estate marked "Private Road", and take the path going uphill. Climb the first set of steps you see on the left to return to the Market Cross.

Notes:

A: **King's Heath** was granted to the burgesses of Malmesbury by King Athelstan, grandson of King Alfred, after the town's men folk helped him defeat the Danes at the Battle of Brunanburh in 937 AD. The 600-acre stretch of land is still held by their descendents The Warden and Freemen of Malmesbury, or the Old Corporation, which also owns many properties in the town.

B: **Corston pond**, an important habitat for toads, was created in the 1950s out of the deepest part of an old limestone quarry. The wildflowers that grow around it from April to September include scabious, oxeye daisies and sometimes orchids. The Local Nature Reserve, the first to be so designated in North Wiltshire, is owned by the Malmesbury St Paul Without Parish Council and maintained by villagers.

3. MALMESBURY CIRCULAR WALK

Distance: 3 miles
Time: $1^3/_4$ hours
Pub: The Smoking Dog, Malmesbury
Map: OS Explorer 168: Stroud, Tetbury & Malmesbury
Star-rating: * Easy

This gentle stroll around the rural fringes of Malmesbury, via Milbourne, brings fine views of this historic hill-top town's distinctive skyline and architecture, dominated by the Abbey. You also see some of the town's splendid buildings, gardens and rivers. The Abbey and the Abbey House Gardens are well worth exploring.

Route:

From the Market Cross, cross the road and walk down the High Street. Half way down turn left into St Dennis Road, then right into Silver Street and then down Back Hill.

Walk 3: Malmesbury Circular Walk

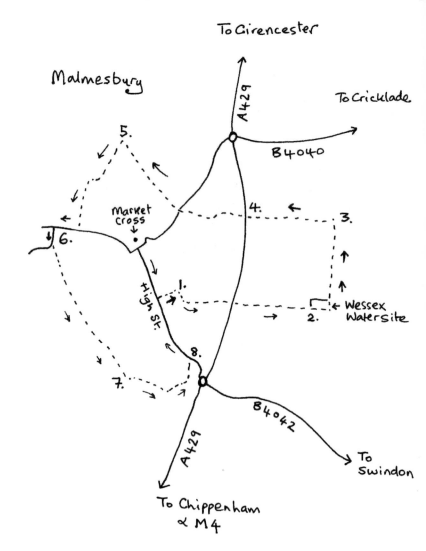

1. At the bottom of the Back Hill steps turn left into Baskerville. Go over Goose Bridge and walk past the bowls club. Continue under the by-pass and over a cattle grid along the metalled drive through a field. Here you are walking parallel with the route of the **Malmesbury branch railway line (A)** on your left.

2. At the end of the drive go over the stile next to the Wessex Water site entrance. Follow the path through the trees and after passing through a gate at the end, turn left uphill. Keep a hedge on your left. At the corner of the field turn left onto a track, go over a stile onto a track and follow this track until it meets a road.

3. Turn left onto the road. Soon you bear left by a phone box onto a No-Through Road. Once through the wooden gate at the end, cross the main road (A429).

4. Continue ahead along Blicks Hill. To avoid walking on the steeply descending road, you can take the footpath to your right – once used by alighting passengers of horse-drawn carriages to lighten the load. Watch out for a wooden kissing gate (near the entrance to a large house) leading onto the footpath. At the T-junction at the foot of the hill, cross the road with care and join the path opposite between a car park and the river.

Frosty morning, Conygre Mead

Once through the wooden gate into Conygre Mead turn right following a path uphill. At the junction of paths at the top, turn right then left across the cricket ground car park. Go over a stile and then follow the footpath along the left edge of the ground behind the club pavilion, and then past the rugby pitch. After another stile, continue downhill. Straight ahead you may see the distinctive undulating roofline of the Dyson building surrounded by tall trees; and to the right the Reeds Farm housing development.

5. At the foot of the hill, take the stile out of the field and turn left. Follow the pavement on the left side of the main road past the supermarket and bus stop over the river bridge. Continue uphill past the mini-roundabout. After about 100 yards, cross the road and walk up the first turning on the right Foundry Road. At the top turn left past some terraced cottages, shortly emerging onto Horsefair. Bear diagonally right across Horsefair then go left along West Street. At the next road junction, turn right onto Bristol Street. On your immediate right you can see a cottage that began life as **St Helen's Church**, believed to date back to the 10th century.

6. Where Bristol Street bends round to the right, turn left down Foxley Road and go over Truckle Bridge. From the bridge and just beyond it, there are fine views up to the crescent-shaped south western edge of the town centre, including the Old Bell Hotel, the Abbey and the bell tower and spire of St. Paul. After passing the river, bear left up a narrow lane past a stile on your left. After passing barns on your right, go through a metal gate ahead of you across the yard, and then over a stile next to another gate. Walk straight on keeping an old hedge on the left, towards a stone building next to a gateway. Go through a gateway and continue in the same direction uphill towards a metal gate. Pass through this and keep going in the same direction keeping a hedge on your left. Go past a gate as the path bends

right to meet a stile in the bottom corner of the field onto Arches Lane.

7. Turn left onto the lane. Over to the right you will soon see the grounds of what used to be **Burton Hill House (B)**. Go past the entrance to Orchard Court on your left and at the next junction, a few yards further on, take the alleyway with metal bars on each side. At a junction of paths, turn right and stay on it through a housing estate. At the end of this, turn left past a red post box into Parliament Row and continue downhill on the pavement.

Plaque showing Malmesbury's historic borough seal, Memorial Gates

8. Take the footbridge, left, over the river and go right through the Memorial Gates to reach a pavement. Turn left up the High Street, which shortly bends round to your right. You soon see the Smoking Dog pub (tel. 01666-825823) on your right. Carry on up the High Street back to the Market Cross and bear left through **Malmesbury Abbey (C)** grounds and past the Old Bell Hotel. Note the brass footplates sunk into the pavement just before Mill Lane, marking the site of the old West Gate. The inscription quotes the poet **John Betjeman**

Malmesbury Abbey

(D) on the "sacred atmosphere" of Malmesbury. Across the road there are views over towards Arches Farm and beyond. Return to the Market Cross via the Abbey grounds or Birdcage Walk near the mirror.

Notes:

A: **Malmesbury branch railway line:** See the notes accompanying Walk 1 Lea.

B: **Burton Hill House** was re-built in the early 1840s. Colonel Charles Miles, who promoted the building of a branch railway to Malmesbury and served on the Malmesbury Railway Company Board, owned the property for many years. From 1936–1945, the house was leased out as a private school. After World War II, the house was sold to the Shaftesbury Society for use as a school for disabled children. This closed in 2007.

C: **Malmesbury Abbey**, and town, owe their origins to a Celtic Monk called Maildulph who in 642 set up a hermitage on top of the hill. The Abbey was founded in 675 by Aldhelm, whose canonisation and shrine attracted pilgrims to the town. Malmesbury was much favoured by Saxon kings as a source of good loyal fighting men ready to take on the Danes. The 14th century stone effigy of King Athelstan lies in the Abbey. Famous for its cloth, silk and wool, Malmesbury also became known in the 17th and 18th centuries as one of the most corrupt of "Rotten Boroughs".

D: In the early 1960s, **John Betjeman** made a short film about Malmesbury in a series of 12 on the West Country towns he loved. Three decades later Gerry Dawson, an HTV producer, unearthed the films. As a result the films have been re-released on video as *The Lost Betjemans*.

4. CASTLE COMBE

Distance:	5 miles
Time:	$2\frac{1}{2}$ hours
Pubs:	White Hart Inn, Ford
Map:	OS Explorer 156: Chippenham
Star-rating:	** Moderate

An enchanting walk through a wooded valley, past clear rushing rivers and streams, and finally into Castle Combe, once voted the most beautiful village in England. The White Hart Inn at Ford and St Andrew's Church are well worth a visit. There are couple of gently sloping inclines. Starts and finishes at Castle Combe – about 10 miles south west of Malmesbury (about 20 minutes drive), via Foxley, Norton and Grittleton.

Route:

From the visitors' car park north east of Castle Combe, walk down the steps to the road, turn right and at the road junction right again towards the village. Continue for about 100 yards.

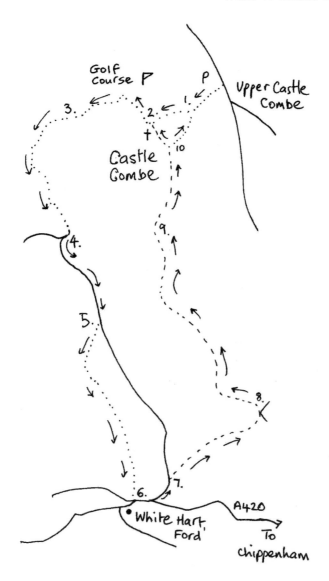

Golf Course **P**

P

Upper Castle Combe

3.

2

1

✝

10

Castle Combe

9

4.

5.

8.

6.

7.

White Hart Ford

A420

To Chippenham

1. Fork right at the walker's sign to Nettleton Shrub into School Lane and go past some houses. Pass between two concrete posts to skirt the left edge of the golf course, keeping a metal fence, and then a stone wall, on your left. Stay close to the wall as the path descends through woods. Ignore the footpath striking off left into the village. There are good views of the church tower and stone roofs of **Castle Combe (A)** a few yards beyond. You soon emerge from woodland onto the Manor House golf course.

Frost on the fairway: the Manor House golf course

2. Continue along the path to join the tarmac drive, turn right and then go left over the stone river bridge. Continue through the golf course and just before another bridge take the path on your left into woodland, keeping the brook on your right. Continue to a metal gate set in a stone surround.

3. After walking a few yards turn left between two houses. At the end of this path turn left and cross the river via a stone bridge and continue uphill.

4. Turn left onto a minor road and continue for about half a mile, with a wooded area falling away steeply to your right. (**Note**: if you need to curtail your walk, there is a **short cut** you can take back to Castle Combe. After passing a sign on your left to Shrub Farm, take the next footpath and descend through woods down to a road. Turn left on reaching the road and walk back into the village). To complete the full version of the walk, continue straight ahead.

5. Just after the next road junction, fork right via a wide metal gate onto a footpath through mixed woodland and then along a hillside down to a brook. Once over a stone stile and a footbridge, bear left into a field and follow the path towards the village of Ford.

6. On reaching the main road (the A420) cross the road with care to visit the 16th century White Hart (tel. 01249-782213), which is signposted. It serves morning coffee and afternoon teas as well as lunches. Otherwise turn left on reaching the main road along the pavement by the road, and take the first road left signposted Castle Combe. (If you visit the pub, retrace your steps to the main road and turn right, then take the first road on your left uphill towards Castle Combe.) After about 250 yards of walking uphill, the road begins to level out.

7. Go over a stile to your right and take the path cutting across the top left side of the hill ahead of you, then down through woods into the hamlet of Long Dean.

8. At the junction of narrow lanes and footpaths, with a red post box ahead, bear left. Stay on this wooded path, part of the **Macmillan Way (B)**, until you reach the southern outskirts of Castle Combe. The path rises gently uphill and then down, with a river on your left.

9. After crossing the stone river bridge, turn right towards the village (past public toilets on your left) along a road. As you proceed through the village note **St. Andrew's Church (C)**, set back from the road, on your left just before the road junction.

10. You have a choice of routes back to the car park.

Cobbled lane, Castle Combe

a) Turn right, between the two pubs, uphill to return via the **Castle Combe Museum (D)**. Take the next left after the museum back up to the car park.

b) To avoid much of the road-walking, and the museum, go straight past the turning to the church, keeping the Castle Inn on your right. Follow the road uphill, beyond the Manor House Hotel entrance, and continue along the footpath under-

31

neath a stone arch. After crossing the stile at the top of the steps, turn right. Here you are back on the same path, bordering the golf course, where your walk began. Retrace your steps back to the visitors' car park.

Notes:

A: **Castle Combe** was transformed into a fictional fishing port for the filming of *Dr Dolittle* (1967), and voted the most beautiful village in England a year later. The Manor House, which dates back to the 14th century, is now a hotel, with a much admired golf course. The Castle Combe motor racing circuit, formerly a World War II airfield, lies about a mile north east of the village.

B: The main route of the **Macmillan Way** long-distance path, running from Boston on the Lincolnshire Coast to Abbotsbury on the Dorset coast, was established to help promote and raise funds for Macmillan Cancer Relief.

C: The parish church of **St Andrew**, dating back to the 13th century, contains some stunning stained glass; and an unusual monument to a Norman knight, Walter de Dunstanville, a great-great-grandson of Henry I of England, who lies in stony, chain-mailed repose with his legs crossed. This posture indicates he fought in two crusades, according to Leonard Lack's short history of the church, (copies may be available for purchase at St Andrew's). Don't miss the glass-encased faceless clock, one of England's earliest timepieces.

D: **Castle Combe Museum** contains a wealth of fascinating old photographs, maps and other artefacts, and opens on Sundays afternoons from Easter to October.

5. LUCKINGTON

Distance:	4 miles
Time:	2 hours
Pubs:	Old Royal Ship, Luckington; Rattlebone Inn, Sherston
Map:	OS Explorer: 168: Stroud, Tetbury & Malmesbury
Star-rating:	* Easy

A relaxing and mainly level stroll south west from the attractive ancient hilltop village of Sherston to Luckington and back. You go through woodland, across farmland, and past the grounds of Luckington Court, featured in the acclaimed BBC TV adaptation of Jane Austen's Pride and Prejudice in 1995. Sherston lies 5 miles west of Malmesbury – about 10 minutes drive – on the B4040. Parking is available in the High Street. A number 41 bus runs between Malmesbury and Sherston, Monday to Saturday.

Route:

Walk along the High Street, **Sherston (A)** away from the church and the Rattlebone Inn (tel. 01666-840871), bearing left behind a stand-alone building (the doctors' surgery) and then down a dip. Take care on the short section lacking a pavement.

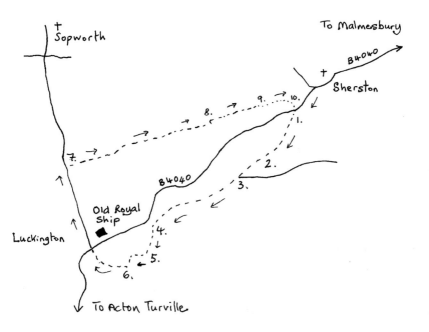

1. Just after crossing the river Avon, take the footpath signed left over a stone stile into a field. At the bottom of the grassy steps bear right and walk along the field edge keeping a post and rail fence, and a river on your left. Nearly half way down the field, cross the river footbridge and then go right through a wooden kissing gate and follow the path as it winds between trees. The

river is now on your right. Soon the path leaves the woodland and takes you into a field.

2. Continue ahead along the path which shortly turns left uphill near a telegraph pole. Where the land begins to flatten out, bear right towards the top corner of the field. Cross over the stone stile into the next field. Bear left across the field and then exit it at the bottom left corner through a gap to reach a lane.

3. Turn right onto this lane. As you approach houses, take the footpath to the right of the ford.

4. At the end of the ford, turn left at the crossroads onto a signposted No-Through Road, continuing through the attractive hamlet of Brook End. On meeting water again, take the footpath to the right of the brook.

5. On reaching a large Cotswold stone house on the right, you see a stone wall ahead of you. Turn right here up towards the church. Just before the entrance to the farm complex, go left through a small wooden gate to walk along a path round the back of the church. As you head for the wooden gate out of the churchyard onto the green, you may see part of **Luckington Court (B)** on your right. As you walk through the green you may be able to see the spire of Alderton church to your left. On

Luckington lion – near St Mary & St Ethelbert church

reaching the end of the green, pass through the gate and cross the road.

6. Turn right and walk along the pavement past the entrance to Luckington Court, on your right. Pass a children's recreation ground on the left and head towards the telephone box. Before crossing the main

37

road to join the Sopworth road ahead, note a splendid example, on your right, of a "tin tabernacle" – Luckington Methodist Church. Then, you will see the **Old Royal Ship (C)** almost immediately on your right on the other side of the main road (B4040). Continue along the Sopworth Road. Follow this quiet minor road for about half a mile until reaching a track on the right (signposted by-way) near the top of an incline.

Tin tabernacle – the Methodist church, Luckington

7. Turn right onto the track and stay on this for nearly a mile.

8. At a T-junction of tracks opposite a wide metal gate, turn left for about 100 yards, and go over the low wooden fence into a large field. Walk straight across the middle of field, going to the right of the remains of a hedge. On reaching the other side of the field go through a gate in the hedgerow and keep going with a hedge, and then a stone wall, on your right.

9. When the wall ends, bear towards the top right corner of the field, and pass through a metal gate. Keep to the right side of the next field. At the edge of a plateau go straight ahead, and down the hill to cross a stone footbridge over the river.

10. Turn right to return to the road, then left up the hill to return to the centre of Sherston.

Notes:

A: Artefacts unearthed in and around **Sherston**, including the remains of a villa, and its proximity to the Fosse Way, suggest a strategic importance in Roman Britain. The unusually wide high street of this former borough boasts several fine 16th century buildings. Sherston hosts

Boules festival, Sherston

its annual Boules Festival, said to be the largest outside France, in July.

B: **Luckington Court** was transformed into the fictional country house of Longbourn in Andrew Davies' memorable BBC TV adaptation, broadcast in 1995 of Jane Austen's *Pride and Prejudice*. The marriage scene was filmed next door – in the Church of St Mary and St Ethelbert, founded by the Abbot of Malmesbury, in 1265 AD. Sir Winston Churchill's "Spymaster", Major-General Sir Stewart Menzies (1890–1968), head of the Secret Intelligence Service during World War II, lived at

Bridges Court, Luckington for most of his life. Known as "C" to his colleagues, Sir Stewart is said to have inspired the fictional intelligence chief "M" in Ian Fleming's James Bond spy thrillers.

C: The **Old Royal Ship** at Luckington (tel. 01666-840222) came to the rescue when the supplier of hot lunches to the village primary school pulled out. Since June 2001, the pub has provided the children's meals.

6. SAPPERTON TUNNEL

Distance: 3 miles
Time: 1¾ hours
Pub: Tunnel House Inn, Coates
Map: OS Explorer 168: Stroud, Tetbury &
                  Malmesbury
Star-rating: * Easy

Visit the source of the Thames, and walk along an old canal towpath to reach the Coates portal of the famous Sapperton Tunnel. The Tunnel House is a super pub, with loads of space to sit outside. This level well-signposted walk starts and ends in Coates, 11 miles (15–20 minutes' drive) north of Malmesbury off the A433 Cirencester-Tetbury road. On street parking available near Coates Village Hall.

Route:

Keep Coates Village Hall and the recycling site on your right as you walk to the end of the road. Go left at the T-junction, signposted Kemble and Tetbury. Cross the road to walk on the grass verge.

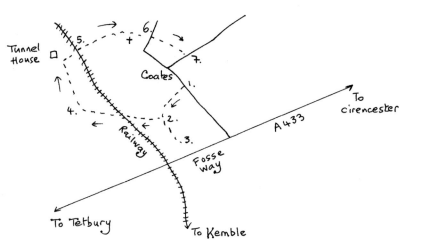

1. After about 250 yards, take the stone stile on the right onto a footpath leading away from the road. Continue alongside the field edge, keeping a stone wall on your right. Go over another stone stile at the far right hand corner of the field, and bear left downhill, with a stone wall now on your left.

2. After passing some farm buildings on your left and once over an old canal bridge you reach a junction of footpaths. Go straight on here, and soon over a stepped stile to the left of a gate, then shortly another. Keep the woodland on your left as you approach a third stile.

3. Once over this walk about 100 yards shadowing the left hand field boundary to reach a simple commemorative

*Round house between Coates
and Tarlton*

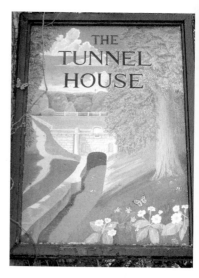

Tunnel House sign

stone marking the **source of the Thames (A)**. Retrace your steps back to the signposted junction of paths by the old canal bridge. Turn left here onto the path adjoining the old **Thames and Severn Canal (B)**, which is part of the Monarch's Way, soon to pass underneath a railway bridge (Kemble to Stroud line). Look out for a derelict **round house (C)** on your left.

4. Where the path forks, take the lower path under a road bridge. As you approach road level, you soon see the

eastern (Coates) entrance – of the **Sapperton Tunnel (D)**.
Go up some steps to emerge opposite the Tunnel House
Inn (tel. 01285-770280). After your refreshment stop,
walk over the tunnel mouth, and then as the drive bends
right, go left over a wooden stile onto a footpath.

5. Walk uphill across a small field to pass over another
   stile ahead. Take great care as you cross the railway
   line and pick up the path ahead leading into a field.

View towards Coates church from the west

45

Walk straight across the field on a path towards a gap in the stone wall ahead of you. On a clear day, away to your right, the Wiltshire Downs and Kemble church spire are visible on the skyline. Continue straight ahead on a grassy path, soon joining a track that passes to the left of farm buildings. Once on a road, go straight on past Coates church on your right soon to reach a T-junction.

6. Cross the road, and pass through a wooden gate opposite. Keep going with trees on your right. Pass through a wooden kissing gate and go straight on in the same direction, keeping a hedge on the right, towards a metal gate and a road back into Coates village.

7. Turn right onto the pavement, passing cottages built for Bathurst estate workers, soon to find Coates village hall again on your right.

Notes:

A: **Source of the Thames:** Barely legible now, the inscription on the commemorative stone reads: "The Conservators of the River Thames 1857–1974. This stone was placed here to mark the source of the river Thames". A few feet in front of the stone lies a hollow where, after heavy rainfall, you may be able to see a few bubbles and the odd puddle. While a few sceptics insist the *real* source of the river is about 11 miles north of here at Seven Springs, near Andoversford, this spot – known as Thames Head – is generally accepted as correct.

B: The **Thames and Severn Canal** was completed in 1789 to link the Stroudwater Navigation with the Thames at Lechlade. The Cotswold Canals Trust (www.cotswoldcanals.com) is working to restore these waterways to navigation after decades of disuse. A similar operation is under way to open up the North Wilts Canal. The plan is to link the North Wilts and the Thames and Severn canals once again at their original junction at Latton, between Cricklade and Cerney Wick.

C: This **round house** was originally a lengthman's home. There were five such homes along this 37-mile long canal, and the lengthmen – as the name suggests – looked after their particular lengths of it. These employees of the canal companies carried out routine maintenance, cut back vegetation, dealt with any leaks and generally watched out for trouble. In the case of the Thames and Severn, each employee would monitor just over 7 miles of canal, living roughly midway along their stretch. There would have been shelter for livestock on the ground floor, living accommodation above, and a cone-like structure at the top for collecting rainwater for drinking.

D: Extending just over two miles, the **Sapperton Tunnel** was once Britain's longest canal tunnel. Boats would have been "legged" through the tunnel – there being no path inside it for horses or people to haul them through.

7. LONG NEWNTON

Distance:	5 miles
Time:	$2\frac{1}{2}$ hours
Pub:	Snooty Fox Hotel, Tetbury
Map:	OS Explorer 168: Stroud, Tetbury & Malmesbury
Star-rating:	* Easy

Well off the beaten track, this mainly level walk from Tetbury to Long Newnton and back, takes you through a largely deserted area of countryside. It includes a stretch of the Fosse Way, and takes you past the former RAF Long Newnton airfield. Tetbury lies about 5 miles north west of Malmesbury along the B4014. To reach the long stay car park, turn right at the first mini-roundabout by the Snooty Fox. Continue along Chipping Street past the short stay car park and turn next right to the old railway yard.

Route:

From the car park follow the pedestrian route, signposted Town Centre via Wiltshire Bridge, passing the old engine shed on your right. Turn left on meeting the main road, then take the footpath that begins on the other side of the hospital entrance, up an incline.

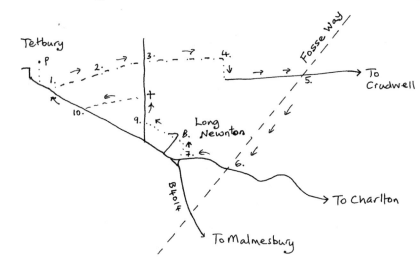

1. Once through the metal kissing gate turn right and continue ahead, keeping a stone wall on your right. As you pass the complex of converted farm buildings, note the 16th century Great Tythe Barn on your right. At the end of the first field, go through another metal kissing gate on your right, and immediately over a stone stile onto a surfaced track. Continue in the same direction straight ahead through a wide farm gate. Once past metal barns on your left, go through the wide gate to your right into a field. Bear left through the field, aiming for a metal gate in the hedge and tree line at the far end.

2. Go through the gate and, bearing slightly right, cross the field towards a pair of electricity poles and a stile set

mid-way in the hedge. Go over the stile into the next field. Carry on, keeping the field boundary of trees and hedgerow on your left. Once past a pond, head for the stile in the left corner of the field onto a road. Cross the road, and pick up the path ahead, through an open gateway.

3. Walk straight ahead shortly into a much larger field, with distant views of the Wiltshire Downs opening up to the right. Continue in the same direction. Bear to the left of a brick pill box, then bend right passing through a gap into the next field. Head towards the tree plantation to the left of the path.

4. Once past the trees, you reach a T-junction of paths. Take the path going right and follow it down to a minor road. Turn left onto the road. Continue past the turning to Boldridge Brake.

5. Take the next right onto the **Fosse Way (A)**, a well-surfaced and shaded section of track. Keep going for about a mile, passing the former **Long Newnton airfield (B)** on your left. Turn right on reaching a metalled driveway.

6. Go right again on reaching a T-junction with a minor road. Continue for about half a mile.

Former Long Newnton airfield – view from the Fosse Way

7. Just before meeting the Tetbury-Malmesbury road (B4014), turn right slightly uphill along a lane marked with a No Through Road sign and head towards a triangular patch of grass. Fork left past this grassy triangle, and follow this lane into a field via a wide gate. Continue straight ahead, sticking to the right hand field boundary, down to a wooden gate. Go through it and continue ahead on the footpath between walls.

8. On meeting a road, cross it and go over the stile ahead into small field. Walk diagonally right across the field, and leave it over a stile in the top corner. Turn left and go through a wooden gate onto a narrow path. (To avoid this field, turn right on meeting the road and follow it round to the left and pass through the wooden gate.)

Holy Trinity Church, Long Newnton

9. On reaching another road, turn right and stay on the verge as far as **Long Newnton Church (C)**. Take the bridleway opposite the church entrance, back towards Tetbury. This path takes you through a strip of land separating two fields. When the bridleway starts curving round to the left, bear right to walk through a wooden gate into a field. Keep the field boundary on your right as you walk down to meet the B4014 Malmesbury-Tetbury road.

10. Cross the road with care and head right along the pavement back to the Wiltshire Bridge, Tetbury. Then cross over the road again and retrace your steps back toward the car park. Just before reaching the car park, take the signposted footpath to the Town Centre via Gumstool Hill to reach the Snooty Fox (tel. 01666-502436) and other refreshment opportunities in Tetbury.

Notes:

A: **The Fosse Way** links Lincoln with Exeter and this section forms part of the county boundary between Wiltshire (left) and Gloucestershire (right). The Romans built this the first arterial road in Britain to link the West Country and the Midlands. On clear days there are good views through gaps in the hedge left towards

Malmesbury and on the horizon the northern foothills of the Wiltshire Downs and the Ridgeway.

B: The only visible remains of **RAF Long Newnton** – a few old ramshackle huts – were requisitioned by the local council after World War II to accommodate homeless families.

C: The blue sundial on the south face of **Holy Trinity Church** tower is well worth a look. The workings and history of the sundial are described in the porch.

8. SHIPTON MOYNE

Distance:	4 miles
Time:	2 hours
Pub:	Cat & Custard Pot Inn, Shipton Moyne
Map:	OS Explorer 168: Stroud, Tetbury & Malmesbury
Star-rating:	* Easy

What connects the first English novel with the Estcourt family, landowners around Shipton Moyne for seven centuries? Find out on this gentle ramble, mainly on the level, through pasture and parkland, and along an attractive river valley. There are fine views towards Tetbury church spire, and on the return leg, the unusual tower of Shipton Moyne church. The walk starts and ends in Shipton Moyne, 3 miles north west of Malmesbury off the B4040 Sherston-Malmesbury road. Once out of Malmesbury take the second turning on the right. Parking is often available in The Street, Shipton Moyne, near the pub.

Route:

Take the waymarked footpath opposite Church Lane, and the village hall in the centre of Shipton Moyne. Walk between two low stone walls, and then go over a stile into a field, and soon over another stile into a second field. Go straight across this field, and over a third stile to reach a fourth one in the hedge ahead. Continue in the same direction, past a plantation on your left.

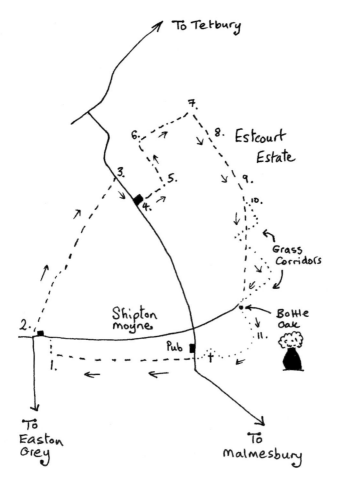

1. Follow the path to the corner of the field, and then turn right following the field edge towards a road. Keep a hedge on your left. Go through a wooden gate next to a stable on your left and turn left onto a lane.

2. After about 100 yards, turn right onto a bridleway next to a stone house called Crossroads. The bridleway can be rather boggy in wet weather. There are good views across the valley on your left about half way down the track. Ignore the footpath striking off left towards Doughton. At the end of the bridleway, cross the road.

3. Turn right to walk along a grass verge towards a pair of semi-detached cottages.

4. Turn left onto a footpath running past the cottages. Go through a wooden gate and soon you should see the spire of Tetbury church in the distance to your left.

5. After passing an old barn, go left through a wide metal gate onto a grassy walkway, and proceed downhill towards a river valley. Go over a stile by a gate and continue down towards a brook and a wooden footbridge. Go over the footbridge.

6. Turn right keeping the brook (sometimes dry) on your right and continue along the floor of the valley through three fields. Go through a wide wooden gate, proceed

ahead and walk uphill to go through a smaller wooden gate.

7. Turn immediately right, and go over the stile, onto a grassy path, with a fence and hedges on the right. After about 30 yards, go through a gate on the right and then down some steps towards the river and a stone footbridge. Then go over a wooden footbridge and a stile into the parkland of the **Estcourt Estate (A)**.

Over the stream, Estcourt Estate

8. Walk uphill keeping a plantation (Thorn Covert) on your right, towards the first in a series of white posts marking the right of way through the estate. Bear right just before reaching the tarmac drive and walk alongside the drive, still keeping the plantation on your right, until you reach a wide wooden gate and a smaller gate next to it.

9. Go through the smaller gate and follow the drive past estate buildings and an old walled garden on your left. After the last house on your right, turn right and soon go over a stile towards fields. (The right of way goes across the fields at an angle. However, to avoid the livestock, walkers are invited to use the grass "corridors" separating the fields.)

10. Go left along a grass corridor here and then on reaching a junction of these walkways, turn right. Soon, go over a stone stile on your left, and turn right. Follow the corridor round to the left, until you meet a second junction of walkways. Turn right at the junction. About 100 yards before a wooden gate directly ahead of you, pass through a small wooden gate to the left and continue along the path until you reach a tarmac drive. (*Detour right here to see an ancient and unusual tree and walk a few yards to a bend in the road. On your right is what's known locally as the "bottle oak". Retrace your steps and head towards a large house.)

11. Just before reaching the house turn right onto path and go through a small wooden gate. Turn left then right towards a stile and gate into a large field. Aim towards **Shipton Moyne (B)** and its church tower with a single turret. Note the double domed roof (left) of **Hodges Barn (C)**. Take the wooden stile (the left one of two close together) out of the field and continue towards the church. Bear right around the church onto Church Lane. You emerge onto The Street by the village hall opposite the Cat & Custard Pot Inn (tel. 01666-880249).

Cat and Custard Pot Inn sign

Notes:

A: The **Estcourt** family lived here from the early 1300s, later ascending to Gloucestershire's landed gentry. In the early 18th century, when England was at war with Spain, **Thomas Estcourt** financed a famous sea expedition to the eastern Pacific to capture Spanish gold. Mariner Alexander Selkirk only survived this violent, scurvy-ridden escapade after being marooned alone for four years on the island of Juan Fernandez – an experience which inspired Daniel Defoe to write *Robinson Crusoe* published in 1719, later hailed as England's first novel. In 1996 the estate passed out of the Estcourt family's ownership: "It's tragic," Desmond Estcourt told *The Times*. "But what's the good of whining? The fact is that I have run out of money." The estate is now a stud owned by Prince Khalid Abdulla's Juddmonte Farms.

B: **Shipton Moyne** appears in the Domesday Book as *sciepton*, meaning "sheep town". It acquired its manorial affix through connections with the Moyne family, whose name is derived from "moigne", a French word meaning monk. The village church features memorials to various Estcourts and to another prominent local family, the Hodges.

Formerly known as the Estcourt Arms, the Cat and Custard Pot's current name dates back at least to 1931.

St John the Baptist Church, Shipton Moyne

It is thought to derive from a reference in R.S. Surtees' book *Handley Cross or Mr Jorrocks's Hunt*, first published in 1854.

C: **Hodges Barn** is a 15th century dovecot converted into a family home. with a six-acre garden – open on certain summer days. Please phone 01666-880202 for details.

9. CERNEY WICK

Distance:	6 miles
Time:	3 hours
Pub:	The Crown Inn, Cerney Wick
Map:	OS Explorer 169: Cirencester & Swindon
Star-rating:	** Moderate

A treat of a walk for all seasons on level ground alongside the Thames and then two linked disused canals undergoing restoration. You pass through North Meadow near Cricklade where thousands of snakeshead fritillaries bloom from late April into May – creating a spectacular display. The walk starts and ends in Cricklade – 11 miles east of Malmesbury, a 20-minute drive along the B4040.

Route:

From Cricklade public car park next to the Town Hall, cross the road and turn right along the High Street pavement passing the splendid Jubilee Clock – on your right by a road junction.

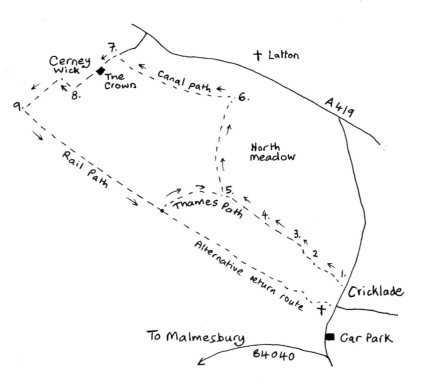

1. Just before reaching the river, turn left along North Wall. After about 30 yards, bear right to join the Thames path, and enter a field. Keep a boundary on your left as you aim for a metal kissing gate across a gap in the tree line ahead in front of some houses.

2. Once through the gap, bear right past houses on your left, go through a metal kissing gate on the right, and

head left across the field. Continue through a metal gate onto a path.

3. Once level with a large barn, turn right over a small footbridge, signposted Thames Path. Follow the path round the back of the barn.

4. Go through a metal gate on your left and continue on the path, keeping the river on your left. You soon enter **North Meadow (A)**. Stay close to the Thames until you

Snakeshead fritillaries, North Meadow, salute the spring

reach a footbridge over the river. Don't cross the bridge. Go over the stile to the right of the bridge, and then turn sharp right, keeping the river behind you.

5. Continue straight ahead along the path, keeping a field boundary on your right (and North Meadow beyond it). As you enter a copse you soon see part of the old **North Wilts Canal (B)** on your left. Carry on over a footbridge until you reach a fence enclosing the grounds of a house. Go right just before the fence, following the path over a wooden footbridge. Continue ahead onto a drive, going over a cattle grid, then a bridge.

6. About 10 yards after the bridge, turn left and go over a stile next to a metal gate to your left. Go straight on following a track for about 50 yards, to an information board. Follow the path as it bends right down a slope towards the main road (A419) soon to bend left. Keep a metal fence and a tree line on your left. Now you have the route of the Thames and Severn canal on your right. On reaching a road, you should see ahead a restored round house or length man's cottage built to house canal workers in the 18th century.

7. Turn left onto the road, soon to reach the Crown Inn (tel. 01793-750369) and a T-junction. Cross the road and the stile next to a signpost. Continue ahead to cross a narrow lane, and pick up the path again straight

Fly takes a break on the canal path east of Cerney Wick

ahead of you. Go through a pair of metal kissing gates. Take the stile to your right into another field, and follow the path with a hedge on your left and a sailing lake – part of the eastern end of the Cotswold Water Park – on your right.

8. At the corner, follow the path round to the right, and soon to the left. After about 100 yards, take a footpath to your left, down some wooden steps over a footbridge into another field. Keep going on the path and exit the

Bridge over the railway path on the way back to Cricklade

field via a stile to join a bridleway – once part of the **Midland & South Western Junction Railway (C)**.

9. Turn left and keep going until you go through a wooden gate across the track. Here you have a choice of routes back to **Cricklade (D)**. You can go left to re-join the Thames Path, and after the footbridge over the river (mentioned at point 4), return the way you came. Otherwise, continue along the railway track to the

outskirts of the town, then follow the National Cycle
Network Route 45 signs, past St Sampson's Church,
back to the High Street. Turn right to return to the car
park.

Notes:

A: **North Meadow**, a 112-acre National Nature Reserve
managed by English Nature since 1973, has the UK's
largest wild population of snakeshead fritillaries. These
delicate wildflowers bloom towards the end of April or
early May. One of England's few remaining ancient
Lammas meadows, unimproved and never ploughed,
this large sweep of lowland attracts a host of inverte-
brates, and aquatic birds.

B: The **North Wilts Canal** opened in 1819 to connect two
pre-existing canals – the Wilts and Berks and the
Thames and Severn. All three are undergoing restoration. Look out for the information boards just past the
house.

C: **The Midland and South Western Junction Railway**, built
in the late 1800s, linked Cheltenham with Andover in
Hampshire. Towns along the route included Cirencester,
Cricklade and Swindon. Enthusiasts have restored one
section of the defunct line to create the Swindon and
Cricklade Railway, on which steam trains run regularly.

D: Founded by King Alfred to help defend the kingdom of Wessex from marauding Danes, **Cricklade** is the most northerly town in Wiltshire, as well as the first town on the Thames. The river was navigable here until the early 19th century. Tourist information is available at Cricklade Town Council, 113 High Street, Cricklade (tel. 01793-751394).

10. EASTON GREY

Distance:	5 miles
Time:	2–2½ hours
Pub:	Cat & Custard Pot, Shipton Moyne
Map:	OS Explorer 168: Stroud, Tetbury & Malmesbury
Star-rating:	** Moderate

An uplifting walk through varied landscape along part of the ancient Fosse Way and past the site of a Roman settlement. Mainly level, the route features farmland, river crossings and a charming Cotswold village mentioned in the Domesday Book. Take refreshments with you or call at the Cat & Custard Pot in Shipton Moyne at the start/ finish. Shipton Moyne lies about three miles north west of Malmesbury, off the B4040 Sherston road. To schedule a pub stop about two-thirds of the way round, you may want to park off-road at the junction of the B4040 and the Fosse Way, and start/finish the walk at that point in step 4 below.

Route:

From the centre of Shipton Moyne, go along Church Lane opposite the Cat and Custard Pot (tel. 01666-880249) and walk through the church gates. Bear left around the church and follow the path to the metal kissing gate at the end of the churchyard.

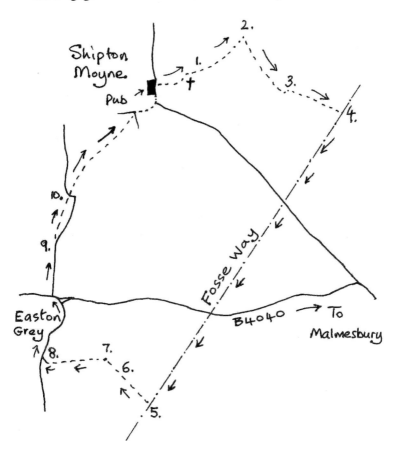

1. Go though the gate onto a grassy path with trees on each side. Continue over the stile near a sundial into a

Heading east from Shipton Moyne through morning mist

field. Follow the path across the field, bearing left of the mature trees in the middle of the field. Cross the stile to the right of a gate, continue to another gate and turn left soon to pass through a smaller gate on your right. Follow the path past trees on your left, go across a drive, then aim for a metal gate at the far right hand corner. Pass through the gate onto a grassy walkway and go straight on until you reach a farmhouse on the left.

2. Look out for a path going off to the right just beyond a gap in the hedge. Take this path and walk downhill between post and rail fences. At the bottom of the hill*, bear left through a narrow wooden gate to walk diagonally uphill aiming for the top far left hand corner of the field and a line of trees. Exit this fenced field via a wooden gate and cross a metalled drive. Head for the stile slightly to your left into a plantation of young trees. (*If there are animals in the field, you can turn left at the bottom of the hill and walk along a grassed track to reach a metalled drive. Turn right onto the drive and walk uphill to meet a line of trees on the left at the top. Take the stile on your left into a plantation of young trees.)

3. Once over this stile bear diagonally right onto the mown path, across a wide gap between the trees, to reach a pair of stiles at the far side of the plantation. Go over these. Bear left and follow the line of some post and rail fencing to reach a stile in a gap in the hedge opposite you.

4. Once over this, turn right to join the **Fosse Way (A)** and continue on it for about two miles. You cross a minor road and later the B4040 Malmesbury to Sherston road. After crossing this second road, the Fosse Way runs close to the eastern edge of what was once a World War II Italian Prisoners of War camp, known as

Easton Grey Camp (B). As you descend towards the River Avon (Sherston branch) note the field on your right – once the Roman settlement of **White Walls (C)**.

5. Immediately after crossing the stone bridge, turn right off the Fosse Way via a wooden stile and continue uphill along the footpath. Approaching the top of the hill, go over a wooden stile at the side of a gate. Keep the hedge on your right all the way to the next stile, and then walk down to a wide gate. Continue downhill and bear left, over the river via a footbridge near a weir.

6. Bear right along a well-defined path uphill through woodland. Emerge into a field and go straight on keeping a hedge on your left. After about 150 yards, pass a gap to reach the corner of the field.

7. Turn left through another gap into the next field and follow the path straight across the middle of it. Ahead, and slightly to the right **Easton Grey House (D)**, set in parkland, may be visible and further right, the tall chimneys of the lodge house near the church. Climb over the wooden stile ahead into a smaller field, and follow the path down towards farm buildings passing through a gate to reach a road. Follow this road round to the right, downhill and emerge into the village at a road junction near a river bridge, thought to date back to the 16th century.

Bridge over the Sherston Avon at Easton Grey

Easton Grey – the view north from the river

8. Turn right and walk uphill through the village, then onto the pavement on the left. Once past the entrance to the lodge house, there is a second set of gates going left leading to **Easton Grey Parish Church (E)**. At the junction with the main road, turn left opposite the bus shelter and almost immediately right across the road to join a lane signposted Shipton Moyne.

9. Once past Church Farm, the lane soon bends to the right. Take the waymarked footpath to the left here through a metal gate and bear right. Head towards a telegraph pole and the spire of Tetbury church. Exit the field before reaching the pole via another metal gate on your right.

10. Cross the road, and the stile in the hedge opposite. Follow the path through this field alongside a line of telegraph poles, aiming for a stile in the fence ahead. Once over this continue in the same direction until you pass the last but one telegraph pole. Go left here (between the last two telegraph poles) and then bear diagonally right to exit the field via a stile in a hedge to reach a road junction. Continue straight ahead, keeping fields and beyond it the church tower on your left into Shipton Moyne.

Notes:

A: **The Fosse Way:** See the notes accompanying Walk 7 Long Newnton for information about the Fosse Way.

B: The observation tower of the WWII **Italian Prisoners of War camp** is visible from the Fosse Way. The inmates painted ornate floral designs onto the walls and ceiling of one particular hut, which they used as their chapel.

C: Excavations of **White Walls** near this spot have yielded several Roman ornaments and coins, jewellery and roof tiles. The settlement serviced and supplied passing traders and imperial messengers between the first and fourth centuries A.D.

D: **Easton Grey House:** A manor on this site was mentioned in the Domesday Book as under the ownership of Roger de Berchelai (later anglicised as *de Berkeley*). Occupants became closely connected, by marriage, with the Hodges family of Shipton Moyne. In the early 20th century, the house was used both by the Duke of Windsor (when still the Prince of Wales) as a base for hunting with the Duke of Beaufort; and by Lord Asquith, Prime Minister from 1908–1916, as a summer holiday retreat. In the 1950s and 1960s, the house hosted a fashion business Peter Saunders Tweeds, relocated from Scotland to Wiltshire. The current 18th century house and gardens were open to the public for many years. Peter Saunders wrote a book *Almost A Fairy Story*, describing the history of the house and his family's connection with it.

E: No known dedication exists for the **Parish Church of Easton Grey**. Its rectors from AD1311–1937 are listed in beautiful script on a wall to the left of the entrance. The tower dates back to the 15th century, although the rest of the church was rebuilt in 1836.

For further information on **Shipton Moyne** and the Estcourt Estate, through which you have passed, see the notes accompanying Walk 8 Shipton Moyne.

11. WESTONBIRT

Distance:	$7\frac{1}{2}$ miles
Time:	4 hours
Pub:	Jack Hare's Bar, Hare & Hounds Hotel, Westonbirt
Map:	OS Explorer 168: Stroud, Tetbury & Malmesbury
Star-rating:	*** More challenging

Lovely parkland, undulating fields, woods, and valleys provide a dream of a walk. You pass the northern fringes of the Highgrove estate, and the extravagant Victorian mansion built by the creator of Westonbirt Arboretum. An optional extension, through the arboretum itself, adds another two and a half miles to the distance above. Starts and finishes at Tetbury, a 10-minute drive (5 miles) north west of Malmesbury. Long stay parking (free on Sunday) and public toilets are at West Street near Tetbury church and Tourist Information Centre (tel. 01666-503552).

Route:

Walk along West Street away from Tetbury church, past Prince of Wales Row, slightly downhill. At the next road junction, turn left downhill along a pavement. Take the footbridge over the stream (sometimes dry) and pass the turning right to Cutwell Farm. Continue along the road for about 200 yards past houses on each side.

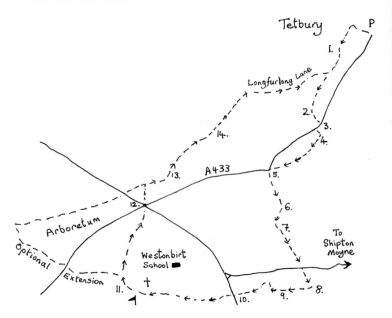

1. After a pair of 30 mph signs, go right into Longfurlong Lane. Just after the lane bends right, take the footpath left over a stone stile. Walking parallel with a stone wall away to the left, follow the path towards a dip and a line of trees ahead. Go over another stile and a wooden footbridge into a field and continue straight ahead, keeping a stone wall and then a hedge on the left.

Footbridge south of Tetbury

2. Just before reaching a small stone store, turn left through a gap between a hedge and the building, then go immediately right, keeping a stone wall on your right. At the corner of the field, go over a wooden stile and then a footbridge to join a road.

3. Turn right onto the pavement and follow it for about 100 yards. Cross the road (A433) with care and take the

83

minor road, signposted Shipton Moyne, which runs alongside Close Nursery.

4. Opposite the nursery entrance take the stone stile right over a wall into a field. Head for the far left hand corner of the field, in a dip, keeping the near clump of trees on your left. At the corner, go left through a gap in the hedge and then turn immediately right onto a track. Continue straight ahead, keeping a ditch and a hedge on your right. At the end of this field continue ahead through an open gateway, keeping a post and rail fence on your left. You soon come level with the rear boundary wall of **Doughton Manor**, which dates back to the 15th century. Go straight on through the farmyard to join a tarmac road.

5. Before meeting the main road, turn left by a notice-board and left again past a new house on your right via a track and then go straight ahead, bearing slightly left, on a footpath through a field towards a line of trees. Continue towards a gap in the hedge, go through it then over a footbridge and across a track. Keep going ahead through the next field with a hedge and trees on your right.

6. Go over a stone stile into another field. Walk diagonally right across the field gently downhill. Go through an opening at the far right corner, just before a wide

wooden gate near a brook (sometimes dry), and then cross over a stone bridge right next to a stone wall. Continue uphill, keeping the mossy stone wall on your right, to reach a wooden gate.

7. Go through this gate and, after a few paces, turn right at a "crossroads" of paths, onto a bridleway, and continue walking with trees on each side. On reaching a road junction, go straight over the road and straight on along a lane signposted Easton Grey.

8. Just after a cluster of houses you reach the entrance to farm buildings, on your right. Here, take the footpath indicated right into a field via a stile. Go straight across the field keeping a line of young trees on your left. Go through a wide wooden gate, and keep going across a field to a smaller gate ahead. Once through this head aim for the far right corner of the field, near houses, and go over a wooden stile next to a metal gate.

9. Go left and through another gate into a farmyard. Stay on the track as it bends round to the right, then left, then right again. Pass the first small turning to your left. After a few paces, on passing out of the farm complex, take the next turning left, by a barn, into a field via a wooden gate. Keep the field boundary and a strip of woodland on your left as you follow the path. Go through a wooden gate. Follow the track round to the

left and then go right, keeping a post and rail fence on the left. Go through another wooden gate into a field. Walk straight over it bearing to the right of some oak trees in the field towards a minor road.

10. Go over a stile, cross the road and take the stone stile ahead into the next field. Keep walking ahead, aiming left of trees ahead. On coming level with the second oak tree, go left through a wide metal gate and then turn sharp right towards a wooden stile (near a water

View towards Westonbirt School from the south

trough), taking you into the next field. Keep the hedge and tree line on your right. Soon you glimpse **Westonbirt School (A)** over to the right. Go through a metal kissing gate into the next field, and keep going in the same direction, aiming for the golf course car park in the distance. Go through a metal gate between a hedge and a wall. Bear slightly right downhill to reach a stile onto the golf course. Aim for the right hand side of the car park and pass through it. Follow the track to join a tarmac road keeping the golf course on your left.

11. After passing through the golf course entrance, you have a choice. To take the **optional extension** through the village and arboretum, see below*. Otherwise, turn right through a wooden gate next to a cattle grid onto a drive through the grounds of Westonbirt School. At a junction with the drive from the main road to the school buildings (right), go straight on. (If the **Westonbirt School Gardens (B)** are open, you may turn right onto this drive to visit them.) Go straight across the drive, bear slightly left, keeping a copse on your right, soon to pass through a metal kissing gate in the fence ahead. Continue in the same direction, through a large field, aiming to pass between two oak trees in the distance. Head for a metal gate next to a line of trees and go through it. Then bear left towards the three-bar metal stile and the main road (A433) beyond which lies the Jack Hares Bar of the Hare and Hounds Hotel

(tel. 01666-880233), and its walled garden. Cross this busy road with care. With the hotel behind you, continue left along a pavement to reach a cross-roads.

12. Cross the road to reach a small wooden gate opposite, amid trees, then another, to pick up a footpath through some paddocks. Keep post and rail fencing on your right. Once over the last stile go straight on to meet a hedge and turn right onto the **Monarch's Way (C)**, keeping the hedge on your left. Continue walking with the hedge and tree line on your left for about 300 yards.

13. Go over the next stile you meet on your left and bear right slightly uphill to cross a stone stile in a hedge. Aim then for the top right corner of the next field and exit via another stone stile. Go right to join a wide grassy track keeping post and rail fencing on your left and a hedge on the right. Go straight on through a gap in a stone wall and continue in the same direction, keeping a hedge on the right. When you reach the corner of this field, go over a stone stile with wooden struts. Go straight across the next field towards a wooden stile. Continue towards a wide wooden gate slightly to the left of a copse.

14. Pass through a wooden gate and then a metal one. Go straight on as signposted, keeping a boundary on your left. Aim for the metal gate in the fence ahead walking

Up and over – Fly negotiates a stile on the Monarch's Way

in the direction of a house. Go through the gate next to the cattle grid by the house. You are now at the south western end of Longfurlong Lane. **Highgrove House (D)**, not visible, is away to your right. Take the first footpath indicated right into a field and turn left downhill to follow the line of the field edge, and going broadly parallel with the lane. Follow the footpath over a series of stiles, finally into a section of woodland. On reaching a stone wall, go left over a stile and bear right across the field to re-join Longfurlong Lane. Turn left at the end of Longfurlong Lane, go over the brook and then turn right into West Street to return to the car park.

Optional extension: Continue ahead through Westonbirt village and straight over the crossroads. Soon, cross over the main road (A433) with care to pick up the bridleway opposite. Stay on this right through the valley floor of the arboretum, finally bearing right

Parish noticeboard and postbox, Westonbirt village

uphill just before the far boundary to reach a wide wooden gate at the top on your left. Go through this and turn right onto the path (part of the Monarch's Way). Keep the arboretum boundary wall on your right, and soon cross a minor road to continue on the path in the same direction. Soon you enter a field. Keep going for about 300 yards, keeping a hedge on your left. Continue as instructed from step 13.

Notes:

A: **Westonbirt House** was the home of the wealthy Holford family for nearly three centuries. The Italian Renaissance style building seen today was constructed in 1863 by Robert Stayner Holford (1808–92) who began the arboretum with a collection of specimen trees planted in the extensive grounds. His son, Sir George Holford, worked with him for more than 20 years to extend the tree collection into Silk Wood, an ancient semi-natural woodland. The 600-acre arboretum, of more than 18,000 specimen trees and shrubs from all over the world, is managed by the Forestry Commission (www.forestry. gov.uk/westonbirt), and supported by the Friends of Westonbirt Arboretum. After Sir George Holford's death, the house became a girls' school in 1928.

B: **Westonbirt School Gardens:** Robert Holford had the entire village demolished and rebuilt a quarter of a mile away in order to accommodate an extension of the gardens. The Grade I Listed gardens are open to the public on certain summer days. To check opening times, telephone 01666-880333.

C: **The Monarch's Way** traces the flight of Charles II after the Battle of Worcester in 1651. Pursued by Oliver Cromwell's army, he travelled north then south through the Cotswolds, the Mendips to the south coast and along the South Downs to Shoreham before escaping to France. The 610-mile long trail links existing footpaths and bridleways.

D: **Highgrove House** was built in 1796–8, and re-built after a fire in 1893. HRH the Prince of Wales bought the house and estate in 1980 from Maurice Macmillan, son of the former Conservative Prime Minister Harold Macmillan. Having embarked on a substantial renovation of the house, the Prince began converting the farm and gardens at Highgrove to organic methods in 1986.

12. LACOCK

Distance:	6 miles
Time:	3 hours
Pubs:	Red Lion, Lacock;
	Lysley Arms, Pewsham
Map:	OS Explorer 156: Chippenham & Bradford-on-Avon
Star-rating:	** Moderate

This delightful route takes you from Lacock through the countryside north east of the village, alongside the old Wilts & Berks canal up to Pewsham Locks and back over Naish Hill. A popular location for film and TV dramas, Lacock featured in Pride and Prejudice, and the Abbey Cloisters in the Harry Potter films. The Lysley Arms, about half way round, serves great food at reasonable prices and has plenty of space inside and out. Lacock lies about 12 miles south of Malmesbury (about 30 minutes drive), off the A350 Chippenham-Melksham road. Follow the signs to the National Trust pay and display car park.

Route:

From the car park entrance cross the road and follow the gravel path. Turn left off the path onto a road into

Lacock, passing the entrance to **Lacock Abbey (A)** and the **Fox Talbot Museum (B)** on your right. Take the first road on the right, East Street, opposite the Red Lion Inn (tel. 01249-730456), and at the end, turn right again towards the church. Once level with the church entrance go left down a No Through Road. Cross the packhorse bridge, bear right along the path past the stream and continue uphill to the top of the lane.

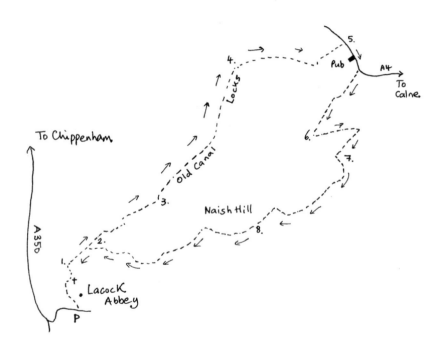

1. Turn right through a wooden kissing gate and walk across a sloping field on the surfaced path. Once through another kissing gate, continue past houses at the hamlet of Reybridge to a road. Turn right and then right again along the stone bridge over the **River Avon (C)**.

2. After about 20 yards, take the stile left and walk diagonally right across the field. Exit the field via a metal stile next to a stone wall. Pick up the footpath on the other side of the road, and continue walking between two fences. Go over another pair of metal stiles into a field. Turn left following the left hand field edge as it bears round to the right. About half way along this long field edge, take the wooden stile to your left into another field. Turn right and keep going with a hedge line on your right uphill soon to enter a thicket.

3. Emerge via a stile, continue straight ahead to join the foot and cycle path. You can now see the route of the **Wilts & Berks Canal (D)** on your right. After a few hundred yards you pass a bend in the River Avon on your left, and a restored canal bridge near a bench. Keep going for about half a mile towards the disused Pewsham Locks.

4. Look out for a footbridge spanning the last disused lock on your right. Cross this and a stile into a field.

Footbridge, Pewsham Locks, south of Chippenham

Keep to the left hand field edge. On the horizon ahead are Derry Hill and the western edge of **Bowood Park (E)**. Continue through a gap into another field. The right of way goes straight across the field to meet a farm track. If the path has disappeared under cultivation, turn left and keep going via the left hand field edge all the way round to meet the farm track. Bear left onto the track and keep going to reach a T-junction with a main road (A4).

5. Turn right onto the pavement. You will soon see the Lysley Arms (tel. 01249-652864) on your right after a garage. Keep going along the pavement and soon enter a cul-de-sac. After walking about 100 yards along this cul-de-sac, turn right by a telegraph pole onto a narrow surfaced lane, also a bridleway, which soon starts winding its way uphill.

6. Just before reaching a big house on the hill, and just before coming level with some garages on your left, turn left to pass through a wide metal gate into a large field. Bear left keeping a wood on the left and a large field rising uphill away to your right, and walk to the corner of the field. Turn right uphill keeping a field edge on your left.

7. Once in the next field, follow the path as it curves left along the field edge and then straightens out as it takes you uphill again. Continue in the same direction.

8. Near the top of the hill, join a farm road via a gate next to a cattle grid and continue to a T-junction. Turn right down Naish Hill and stay on the lane all the way back to the bridge over the Avon which you crossed at the end of point 1. Retrace your steps back into Lacock the way you came. You will see the Red Lion opposite the junction of East Street with the High Street. There's a National Trust café next to the pub.

South end of East Street, Lacock

Notes:

A: **Lacock Abbey:** Built for an order of Augustinian nuns, the Abbey became a family home after the Dissolution, and was donated to the National Trust by descendants of the Fox Talbot family in 1944. The Cloisters have featured in several Harry Potter films.

B: **Fox Talbot Museum:** Housed in a 16th century barn, the museum celebrates the life and work of Lacock's most famous resident William Henry Fox Talbot, who came to live at the Abbey in 1827. He invented the negative-positive photographic process, and used architectural features of the Abbey in many of his first photographic experiments.

C: **The River Avon:** Avon is an old English word meaning river. This is part of the Wiltshire Avon, which rises above Malmesbury (the Tetbury and Sherston branches meet east of Baskerville, Malmesbury) and meanders down through Wiltshire and Somerset, via Chippenham, Melksham and Bath to the sea at Avonmouth, west of Bristol.

D: Built between 1795–1810 to connect the Thames at Abingdon with the Kennet and Avon Canal at Semington, the **Wilts and Berks Canal** (www.wbct. org.uk) is undergoing restoration for public access after falling into disuse nearly a century ago.

E: **Bowood Park:** About 100 acres of parkland surrounds Bowood House (www.bowood.org) the family seat of the Marquis and Marchioness of Lansdowne. Open to the public from April to October, the Bowood estate includes landscaped gardens designed by Capability Brown, a rhododendron walk and a much-praised children's adventure playground.

13. LITTLE SOMERFORD

Distance:	6 miles
Time:	3 hours
Pubs:	Rose & Crown, Lea;
	The Saladin, Little Somerford
Map:	OS Explorer 168: Stroud, Tetbury &
	Malmesbury
Star-rating:	** Moderate

Rich in railway interest, this walk from Malmesbury to Kingsmead Mill on the western edge of Little Somerford takes you via Lea and back past Cole Park. Mainly level, the route offers an optional extension into the centre of Little Somerford which adds two miles.

Route:

From the Market Cross, Malmesbury, and facing the High Street, turn left along Oxford Street. At a T-junction in front of Tower House, cross the road and turn right soon to pass the short stay car park (right) and the library (left). A few yards further on, turn left down Silver Street, past Ingram Street and go down the Back Hill steps.

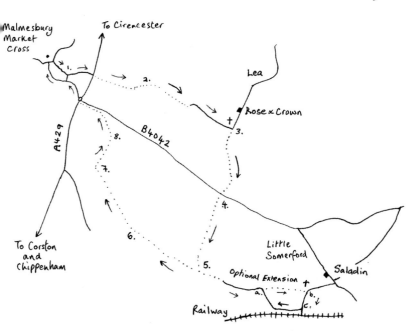

1. Turn left, go over a river bridge and pass the bowls club on your left. As the road bends right – and just beyond a house called Watersmeet – the Sherston and Tetbury branches of the Avon join. At the end of the road, pass to the right of a wide metal barrier and continue in the same direction underneath the A429 Malmesbury by-pass on a tarmac lane. Go over a cattle grid (or through the gate next to it) into a field. Continue ahead on the lane. Watch out for occasional vehicles. Where the lane bends left, note some remains of a railway bridge (left)

once part of the Malmesbury branch line. Carry on to reach a Wessex Water site entrance.

2. Turn right just before the entrance and go through the gate or over the stile on the right to join a narrow tree-lined path running past the side of the sewage works. Go through a metal gate at the end of this path into a field. Keep going in the same direction, gently uphill, keeping a hedge on your right. After the ground levels out you soon reach a stile on the right next to the end of the hedge. Cross the stile and walk downhill aiming for a bend in the farm lane visible near the bottom left corner of the field. Go through a wooden gate by the river to join the farm lane. Turn right and follow it as it bends left soon to pass between buildings. Stay on the lane through a field and then past some houses on the outskirts of Lea.

On reaching a T-junction, turn left onto a pavement, cross over the entrance to Pembroke Green and pass St Giles Church. When you come level with the back of the church, you have a choice. If visiting the Rose & Crown pub (tel. 01666-824344) follow the pavement round to the left past the back of the church, and you will see the pub and garden on your left. If not visiting the pub, turn right, and cross the road to join a footpath via two white posts set at angle, near a yellow grit store.

Pigeon in the tower – St Giles Church, Lea

3. Continue along this narrow path soon to enter a field via a stile. Turn left and keep a boundary on the left for about 60 yards. Take the stile on your left set in a field boundary, then turn right onto a path running between a double row of young trees (left) and a hedge (right). After crossing the next stile, walk diagonally left across a field along a clear path and go over the next stile into another field. Walk uphill – keeping a hedge on the left – and soon pass an electricity pole (left). Go through a metal gate next to a tree at the corner of the field and turn left. Ignore another metal gate on the left and walk a few paces towards a section of post and rail fence (three horizontal wooden rails and a large oak post) Climb over this, turn right and carry on keeping a barbed wire fence on the right. Head towards farm buildings along a grass strip and go left at the corner. Go through the first metal gate you see on your right, then another to join a track through a farmyard soon to reach a T-junction with the B4042 (Malmesbury-Swindon road).

4. Cross the road and continue along the track opposite leading to **Maunditts Park Farm (A)**. On a clear day, there are fine views on the right towards the Severn Vale and the Rodbourne water tower. Continue straight ahead following the track into a large sloping field, through a gate into a second field where the ground becomes level. Continue to a gap in the trees ahead to reach a T-junction with part of the route of the dismantled Malmesbury branch railway. Turn left here to pass along the disused railway route, and continue for about 60 yards. Turn right over a wooden footbridge. Continue straight ahead, keeping trees on your right at first, then post and rail fencing. As the path bends left, you pass a small copse on your left and see a bridge away to your right. Soon you reach a junction of paths, with a metal fence ahead of you and the river Avon just beyond it. Here you have a choice: to do the **optional extension*** into the centre of Little Somerford, adding two miles to your walk, see the directions below. If not doing the extension, turn right

here either through the gate or over the stile on your right.

5. Turn left and follow the river to a bridge. Turn left over the bridge via gates at each end. Follow a clear path soon to pass a large bend in the river on your right. You soon enter a clearing, passing between two lines of young trees, to emerge by a metal gate. Go through this into a large field and continue ahead, slightly left, towards a wide gap in the trees in the distance. Walk

View across the Avon from the footpath west of Kingsmead Mill

through the gap (it can be boggy at this spot next to the river), straight across the next field and aim for the far left corner. Go through a wooden gate in the corner and then over a stone footbridge across a junction of streams. Bear left, keeping a bend in the stream on your left. Where the stream straightens out, turn right across a field towards a wooden gate in the tree and hedge line.

6. Go through the gate and walk straight ahead up a gentle incline, keeping a hedge on your right and the cultivated area of a large field on your left. Go through a gap in the tree line ahead into the next field where the gradient becomes slightly steeper. Continue in the same direction through another gate, over the brow of a hill and then straight on downhill past the ha-ha separating the gardens of **Cole Park (B)**, away to your right, and the field. If there is electric fencing across the path near the ha-ha, you can step over the sheathed sections. Go over a stile into the next field, and continue straight on across a drive and over another stile in the fence ahead of you. Walk straight across the field, past some tall trees on your left, aiming for the right hand side of a tall evergreen hedge near farm buildings. On reaching a junction with a track, turn right along it, and go through a gate.

7. Keep going on the track uphill with a hedge on the left, then once through a gateway, down the other side of the hill. Towards the bottom of the hill, just past a large

oak tree near the hedge on your left, go across a stile in the hedge-line on your left. Continue along the bottom edge of the field. After passing the first large tree on your left, go over the stile on your right, and then a second one, to emerge into a sloping field.

8. Go straight along the top edge of the field, keeping a hedge on your left, towards the roofline of a large house. Go over a stile near the corner of the field and bear diagonally left uphill, passing a small fenced area of young trees on your left, to reach a stile at the brow of the hill. Cross the stile into the next field. Follow the path gently downhill aiming well to the right of the new health centre and care home complex ahead. Pass through a wide wooden gate set in the fence ahead of you into the next field. Go diagonally right across the field and go over a stile in the corner. Go straight on, keeping a boundary on your right, over one last stile to join a track that takes you down to the main road (A429). Cross the road and bear right along the pavement. Go straight on across the entrance to Barley Close, and continue downhill passing houses on both sides, then the back of a bus shelter on the right. Just before reaching the road bridge, turn left onto a footbridge over the river, then turn right through a pair of wrought-iron gates. Turn left onto the pavement and walk along the High Street which soon bends right and takes you back up to the Market Cross.

* **Optional extension** Turn left at the junction of paths
and keep going with the metal fence, and beyond it the
river, on your right. Soon a high stone wall appears on
your right, replacing the fence. After passing across a
driveway keep going with a grass bank on your right
and a track on the left. Go through a metal gate to
emerge at the end of a lane. Beyond the gates on your
right lies **Kingsmead Mill (C)**. The Little Somerford
railway viaduct stretches across the horizon ahead of
you beyond some young trees. Turn left onto the lane
and go past the former (railway) crossing-keeper's
cottage on the left and over the site of **Kingsmead**

Railway viaduct from the western end of Mill Lane

Crossing (D). Continue uphill under a tree canopy to reach a junction with a drive to a house on the left and a stile ahead of you into a field.

a) Go over the stile and straight across the field to climb over a section of post and rail fencing into a second field. If the right of way is unclear across this field, turn right and keep a boundary on your right. At the corner of the field turn left, keeping the boundary on your right. After about 100 yards, go over a stile next to a gate on your right. Aim for a high wooden fence ahead of you, soon to pass to the right of a pond. Keep the church tower in your sights as you aim for the far left corner of the field. Take the wooden stile to the left of a house and then cross a pair of stiles. Continue ahead on a narrow footpath all the way to a road.

b) Turn left to reach the centre of Little Somerford. St John the Baptist Church soon appears on your left. The church contains a memorial to a famous balloonist Walter Powell, who was elected MP for Malmesbury in 1868. Powell was lost over the English Channel in the balloon Saladin in December 1881, never to be seen again. To reach the Saladin pub (tel. 01666-824222), continue past the church to reach a T-junction about 400 yards further on. Turn left at the junction and you will soon see the pub on

Village sign, Little Somerford

your left. Retrace your steps past the church and the footpath you walked on earlier.

c) Just before reaching the railway bridge over the road, turn right into Mill Lane, passing the village hall on your right. Stay on Mill Lane past the former crossing-keeper's cottage, and retrace your steps past Kingsmead Mill all the way back to the spot where the optional extension begins. Go straight on over the stile or through the gate, and continue as described from point 5 above.

Notes:

A: Maunditts Park is thought to be of Norman origin and named after John Mauduit, Sheriff of Wiltshire and

Governor of the Castle of Old Sarum in the reign of Edward III. It was a deer park for about three centuries from this time until Charles I's reign.

B: Originally owned by Malmesbury Abbey and known as Cowfold, **Cole Park** is a moated medieval manor house, parts of which date back to the latter half of the 16th century. After the Dissolution, the estate was granted to Edward Seymour, Duke of Somerset in 1548 and for much of the Tudor period it was a royal stud farm. The family of Hugh Audley, Sheriff of Wiltshire in 1654, owned it during the 17th century.

C: **Kingsmead Mill** operated as a working mill for many years under the ownership of the Fry family until 1961. Subsequent owners have included the film maker (Lord) David Puttnam, and the bagless vacuum cleaner inventor Sir James Dyson, Malmesbury's biggest employer.

D: **Kingsmead Crossing** was the mid-point of the Malmesbury branch railway line from Dauntsey Lock. Bill Archard became crossing keeper in 1922 and he lived at the cottage until 1979. The crossing keeper's cottage remains. See the notes accompanying Walk 1 Lea for more information about the Malmesbury branch railway.

14. AVEBURY

Distance:	4 miles
Time:	2 hours
Pub:	Red Lion, Avebury
Map:	OS Explorer 157: Marlborough
Star-rating:	* Easy

A relaxing walk through quintessential Wiltshire landscape finishing with a visit to the ancient stone circle, at the heart of the World Heritage Site. From Windmill Hill there are captivating views in all directions, notably of the Ridgeway, Silbury Hill, Cherhill Down and the Earl of Lansdowne monument. Starts and finishes at the visitors' car park (pay and display, free to National Trust members) in Avebury – about 10 miles south of Swindon off the A4361 Marlborough Road.

Route:

From the visitors' car park in Avebury, head towards the village along the waymarked footpath. Turn left when you reach the road, then right just past the church entrance, and at the end of that, left again onto a narrow lane. After passing a pumping station on the left, look out for Silbury Hill on your left, and go over a footbridge.

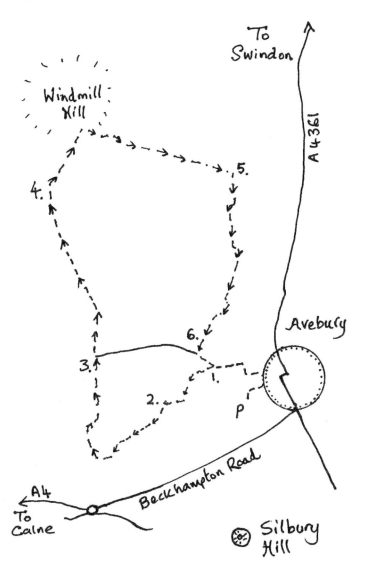

To
Swindon

A 4361

Windmill
Hill

4.

5.

6.

3.

2.

Avebury

P

Beckhampton Road

A4
To
Calne

Silbury
Hill

1. Where the footpath forks, take the left fork onto a section of the **Wessex Ridgeway (A)**. Go through the gate into a field and follow the metal fence on your left to exit the field near a house. Continue to a junction of tracks at **Avebury Trusloe (B)**.

2. Go straight on, and on reaching another road, continue straight ahead along a footpath through a pair of metal bars. At the end of this turn right onto a narrow road, and continue ahead past some cottages. **Longstones**

Adam and Eve stones, Longstones Field, Avebury Trusloe

Field (C), excavated by a team of Southampton University archaeologists in 1999, soon appears on the right. Continue past two standing stones – the Adam and Eve stones – and follow the track round to the right, skirting the edge of the same field.

3. After passing between two barns, go straight on at the junction of tracks to start ascending **Windmill Hill (D)**. As you approach the summit you get a better view of the Ridgeway over to your right, and of Cherhill Down and the Earl of Lansdowne monument, to the left. Soon you reach a gate on the right and a National Trust sign, marking the entrance to Windmill Hill.

4. Pass through the gate, and walk towards the right of the summit. Continue to the other side of the field in the same direction to another gate and a second National Trust sign. Go through the gate and walk downhill keeping a metal fence, and later a hedgerow, on your left. Pass through a metal gate.

5. Just after the grass gives way to a tarmac track, take the footpath signposted right into a field back towards Avebury. Cross to the next field via three stiles close together in a hedgerow. Continue in the same direction until you reach a footbridge. Cross this and turn left towards a stile ahead of you.

Lychgate and church tower, Avebury

Part of the Avebury stone circle and World Heritage Site

6. Turn left along the path and retrace your steps back into Avebury.

   To visit the Red Lion (tel. 01672-539266) continue past the path leading back to the car park. The pub is at the top of the road on the left. Access to the stone circle is via several gates around the village.

Notes:

A. **Wessex Ridgeway:** This 136-mile route from Marlborough to Lyme Regis was devised by the Ramblers' Association in the mid 1980s. It joins the Ridgeway National Trail – an 85-mile route from nearby Overton Hill to Ivinghoe Beacon, Buckinghamshire – about two miles north east of Avebury.

B. **Avebury Trusloe:** After the heir to a Scottish marmalade fortune Alexander Keiller bought much of the village in the 1930s, and embarked on his famous excavations of the circle, many of the older cottages within it were demolished. It was decided that new buildings should be restricted to Avebury Trusloe in order to protect the integrity of the stone circle.

C: **Longstones Field:** William Stukeley, an 18th century antiquarian, proposed the existence of a prehistoric "Beckhampton Avenue" of paired megaliths into the

Avebury stone circle, similar to the West Kennett avenue still evident today to the east of the village. An excavation here by the Southampton University team in 1999 provided the best evidence to date that Stukeley was right. They found evidence of three buried stones, and three pits where stones had either been removed or burned. (The next featured walk around Silbury Hill takes you through West Kennett Avenue.)

D: **Windmill Hill:** The site of the earliest-known Neolithic settlement in the area, dating back about 5,500 years, Windmill Hill was revealed during excavations in the 1920s by Alexander Keiller and others as a causewayed enclosure. Evidence suggests that these early settlers – the Beaker People – kept cattle, sheep, pigs, goats and dogs, grew crops and made pottery.

15. SILBURY HILL

Distance:	5 miles
Time:	2½ hours
Pub:	Red Lion, National Trust café, both at Avebury.
Map:	OS Explorer 157: Marlborough
Star-rating:	** Moderate

Rich in prehistoric sites, spectacular downland views, and landscape interest, this is a rewarding walk all year round. You may see a crop circle in the summer. The hay and straw bales in the fields at harvest time complement the ancient standing stones. Mainly level with one or two moderate inclines. Park at the National Trust visitors' car park off the A4361 at Avebury.

Route:

Turn right out of the car park away from the village. After 20 yards cross the main road opposite a signposted footpath. Pass through a wooden gate and continue on this path with a fence on your left and a stream running along a ditch on the right. Pass through a pair of gates, from which **Silbury Hill (A)** is visible on the right; then cross over a pair of stiles. Continue in the same direction to meet the main road (A4).

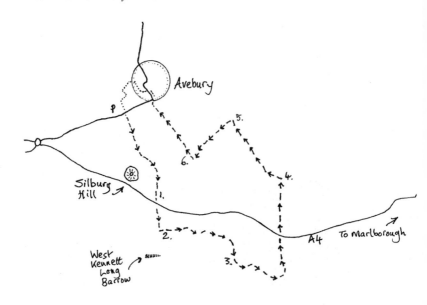

1. Cross the road with care, turn left and almost immediately right onto a path.

2. After going over a bridge, go left through a kissing gate keeping a field and a hill on your right. If you wish to visit the **West Kennett Long Barrow (B)**, turn right at the corner of the field and walk straight up the hill. If not continue straight ahead on the path.

Go straight on over a minor road, keeping a field boundary on your right. Soon you cross a stile into a small woodland.

120

Silbury Hill from the A4 near West Kennett Long Barrow

3.   At a T-junction of paths turn left onto a bridleway. On
     reaching a road, turn left, go over a bridge, and then
     almost immediately right. Keep to the field edge on
     your right. When you reach another T-junction of
     paths, you should see the tower of West Overton church
     ahead. Turn left uphill. Before crossing the main road
     (A4), look out for the site of a prehistoric shrine called
     the **Sanctuary (C)** on your left, and a good view of
     Silbury Hill. Once over the road continue on the track
     up Overton Hill, past three burial mounds on your
     right. This point marks the start of the ancient
     Ridgeway (D).

4. Take the first path left, signposted a by-way. Once past a stand of beech trees, you should be able to see the tower of Avebury church ahead and the West Kennett stone avenue away to your left. Continue downhill on the path for about 1/4 of a mile. Then the path starts rising gently uphill.

5. After about 150 yards of gentle uphill walking, take the footpath left along a field edge, keeping a fence on your right, soon to reach a road. Cross the road and pass through the wooden gate on the right.

6. Turn right and pass through **West Kennett Avenue (E)**. At the end of the Avenue, cross the road again, to pass through a gate leading to the Avebury stone circle. Follow the henge round to your left to reach the Red Lion pub (tel. 01672-539266). Alternatively bear left and follow the line of the road, to cross it once more half way down the field. This takes you into towards the centre of the village, the National Trust restaurant and shop, public toilets, Avebury Manor and the Museum.

Notes:

A: **Silbury Hill:** At around 40 yards high, this is Europe's largest man-made pre-historic mound. Several early Wiltshire writers link its origins to the nearby rising of the River Kennet at Swallowhead Springs, a few

Walkers on the bank above the stone circle, Avebury

hundred yards to the south. Others suggest that it was built as a monument to the Celtic goddess Sul, or – as a giant sundial.

B: **West Kennett Long Barrow:** One of the best known and most visited of the Neolithic earthen mounds constructed for multiple burials. A bigger one is at East Kennett, unexcavated and lacking a right of way to it.

C: **The Sanctuary:** Some 5,000 years ago a timber shrine was erected here. It was later replaced by a double stone circle, linked by an avenue of stones to a new temple at Avebury.

D: **The Ridgeway** stretches from Overton Hill near Avebury to Ivinghoe Beacon in the Chilterns. It was used as a drovers' road or trading route at least since the bronze age. An 85-mile long national trail, incorporating most of the ancient road, was created in the early 1970s.

E: **West Kennett Avenue** is widely supposed to have been built as a processional route for Neolithic people visiting Avebury for ritual gatherings; and that the alternating shapes of the standing stones, upright columnar stones then wide, flat ones, represent male and female figures.

16. ASHTON KEYNES

Distance:	6 miles
Time:	3 hours
Pubs:	Baker's Arms, Somerford Keynes;
	White Hart Inn, Ashton Keynes
Map:	OS Explorer 169: Cirencester & Swindon
Star-rating:	** Moderate

Riverbanks, lakes and abundant wildlife are the themes of this tranquil walk on level paths through part of the Cotswold Water Park from Somerford Keynes to Ashton Keynes via the Thames path. Plenty of bird-spotting opportunities. The walk starts and finishes at Neigh Bridge Country Park car park, near Somerford Keynes, a 15-minute drive (8 miles) from Malmesbury, via Crudwell and Oaksey.

Route:

From Neigh Bridge Country Park car park pass between the information board and the public toilets, and bear right before a children's play area. Keep the lake on your left and soon enter woodland to pick up the Thames Path. Once on the path, you see the lake through trees on your left and the river on your right.

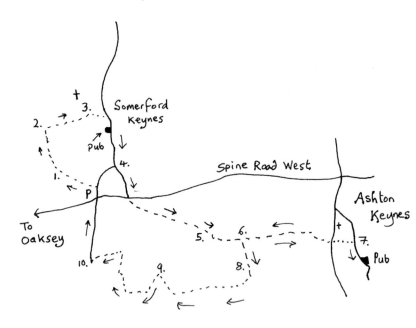

1. At the far end of the lake turn right off the lakeside path over a wooden footbridge into a field. Follow the left hand field edge keeping the hedge and river on your left. The path soon bends to the left. At the end of the field go through a gate. Ignore a footbridge going over the river to Kemble Mill, and instead keep going straight on until you reach a clear grassed path on your right going straight across the middle of the field.

2. Take this right turn across the field. After a bend to the right, take the footbridge left and enter parkland. Go straight ahead and in the middle of the field, bear slightly left to follow the path to a gate.

3. On reaching the corner of the field just to the right of the church, pass through a wooden gate and follow the footpath ahead. Continue along the footpath keeping a high stone wall on your right, and a row of young trees on your left. Turn left onto a gravel drive past cottages onto a road. Turn right onto a pavement to walk

Lakeside homes, Lower Mill Estate, viewed from Thames Path

through Somerford Keynes village. The Baker's Arms (tel. 01285-861298) is on the right.

4. As the road bends right, turn left into Mill Lane and at the end cross the main road to pick up the lane opposite. After a few yards, turn left onto a lakeside path. The lakes you see on this walk form part of the **Cotswold Water Park (A)**. Soon, on your right you pass some of the second homes built on the **Lower Mill Estate (B)**. At the end of the path, join the tarmac road for about 20 yards then continue ahead on the track.

5. On approaching a wooden gate ahead, cross the metal footbridge on your right over the Thames and follow the path as it bends left.

6. At a junction of footpaths, continue straight ahead towards Ashton Keynes. (To shorten the walk by a couple of miles, you can turn right here, following the path signposted to Poole Keynes, picking up the route from point 8 below.) Cross over a road and continue towards **Ashton Keynes (C)**, keeping the river on your left.

7. On reaching a T-junction, turn right to reach the White Hart Inn (tel. 01285-861247), which has a pleasant garden. Retrace your steps back along the Thames Path

Morning frost on the banks of the Thames at Ashton Keynes

to the junction of footpaths mentioned above at point 6. Turn left to follow the signposted Poole Keynes path.

8. Stay on the track between a lake on your right and a hedge on your left. You are walking along the eastern edge of the Lower Mill estate nature reserve. Follow the track, which soon bends right towards a wooden footbridge. After crossing the footbridge, follow the

Belted Galloway cattle, Lower Mill Estate

footpath as it bears right across a meadow keeping a fence, and just beyond it Swill Brook, on your left.

9. On reaching another footbridge follow the waymarked path through woods and the **Swillbrook Lakes Nature Reserve (D)**.

10. On reaching a road, go through the kissing gate and turn right along a quiet road. At the junction with the

spine road, cross over the road to return to the Neigh Bridge Country Park car park.

Notes:

A: The **Cotswold Water Park** (www.waterpark.org) is the largest of its kind in the UK – bigger than the Norfolk Broads – and still growing. More than 130 lakes have been created, out of former gravel pits, across 40 square miles. A haven for wildlife, it offers a wealth of leisure and educational opportunities – water sports, cycling and walking, angling, bird-watching and conservation activities.

B: Described by one commentator as a "brave new ghetto for weekenders...an exercise in social engineering", **Lower Mill Estate** claims to be the UK's first "residential nature reserve". Former publishing tycoon Jeremy Paxton's innovative development combines entrepreneurial flair with a passion for the environment, wildlife and conservation. www.lowermillestate.com.

C: **Ashton Keynes** is an attractive little village with dainty footbridges spanning the shallow Thames. Refugees from Nazi Germany and elsewhere in mainland Europe fled here in the 1930s to form the Cotswold Bruderhof, also known as the Hutterian Brethren. A closed community of pacifist Christians, they farmed 300 acres for many years and lived a simple, frugal life. Ever resourceful, they built a power station and hospital and carried out printing and bookbinding. In the 1940s, the Community relocated to Primavera, a rural backwater of Paraguay.

D: **Swillbrook Lakes Nature Reserve** provides flourishing habitats to a host of summer migrant and over-wintering birds, dragonflies and damson flies, and wildflowers. The reserve is run by the Wiltshire Wildlife Trust. (www.wiltshirewildlife.org).

17. AVENING

Distance:	6 miles
Time:	3 hours
Pubs:	Weighbridge Inn, nr. Nailsworth; Bell Inn, Avening
Map:	OS Explorer 168: Stroud, Tetbury & Malmesbury
Star-rating:	** Moderate

Gently undulating countryside with plenty of woodland shade make this a good walk for all seasons. Pleasant views towards Gatcombe Park, home of the Princess Royal, on the return leg. Starts and finishes in the attractive village of Avening, whose church and churchyard are well worth a visit. Parking is available in Avening High Street. The village lies 3 miles north of Tetbury on the B4014, and is within about 15 minutes drive from Malmesbury.

Route:

From the Post Office and stores in Avening High Street, walk downhill and take the first turning left Point Road just before a phone box. Ignore the turning to Pound Hill and continue to a T-junction. Turn left and follow the road as it narrows to a single-track lane, soon passing a No Through Road sign. There are good views right across the valley.

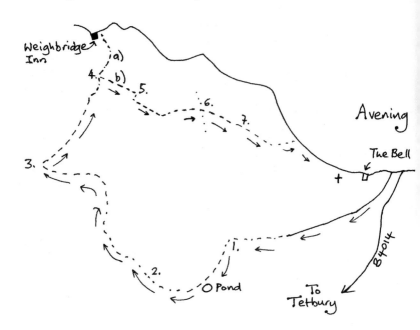

1. At the bottom of the hill, go past the bridleway waymarked to the left, but take the next footpath to the left a few paces further on along a tarmac drive. About 50 yards after leaving the road, take the footpath diversion to your left through a wooden gate. Turn right onto a grassy path. Go over a wooden footbridge ahead, and then a stile with a dog door to the side.

Farm and hillsides, east of Avening

Turn left, keeping a stream on your left. Follow the footpath along the bottom of the valley, with a hedge and trees on your left. Keep going past a pond (left) as the path bends right.

2. Continue straight towards trees ahead and pass through a gate. The path rises gently uphill with a plantation on your right. Follow the footpath signs across fields,

135

keeping a boundary on your left, before reaching a junction of paths in a wooded area.

3. Turn right onto a track (marked on the OS map as Shipton Graves Lane) and continue along this, mostly through woods. You may be able to see the Wiltshire Downs on the distant horizon (right). If the track is very muddy there is an alternative parallel track through the woods on your right. Half a mile further on, at a second junction of paths, bear left through the second metal gate on the left (with a blue arrow marker on the gatepost). On reaching another patch of woodland, Hazel Wood, you reach a third junction of paths.

4. Here you have a choice:

   a) To visit the Weighbridge Inn (tel. 01453-832520), about 10 minutes walk from here, go straight on downhill, following a track that borders a small stream. Go straight across a field, keeping to the right of the stream, and then back into woodland, towards a road. If the track is muddy, there are alternative paths either side. Go through a metal gate onto a road. Cross the road with care, and turn left onto a pavement. The pub is about 20 yards down the road to your left. Retrace your steps back to the crossroads of paths and go left just before the gate.

Pub sign, The Weighbridge Inn

b) If you are not visiting the pub, simply turn right at the junction of paths. Now you have Hazel Wood on your left and a field on the right.

5. Follow the signs through the wood. Cut right soon, via a wooden kissing gate, then round to the left to pass fields on the right. After about quarter of a mile, fork left, as indicated, back into woodland to re-join the track you walked on earlier.

6. At the next junction of tracks, go straight ahead downhill through a wide metal gate. Continue on the track downhill with a few trees on the left and a grassy bank rising to the right. Keep going on the track

between oak trees. On reaching farm buildings, go through a metal gate and continue straight ahead through another gate into a field.

7. Continue in the same direction across the field to pass through a third gate onto a narrow path. Keep a stone wall on your left and a hedge on the right. There are fine views on your left towards **Gatcombe Park (A)**, home of HRH the Princess Royal. Soon you join a wider track coming from your right. Continue walking downhill back into the village. Turn right back into Avening High Street. Just before the Bell (tel. 01453-836422) turn right to pass the school if you wish to visit **Holy Cross Church (B)** and **Churchyard (C)**.

Notes:

A: **Gatcombe Park**. The manor house was built between 1771–74 for Edward Sheppard. In 1979, the Queen bought the house and 730-acre estate for Princess Anne and Captain Mark Phillips. The royal couple hosted the first Gatcombe horse trials here in 1983. The Princess Royal now lives in the manor with her second husband Rear-Admiral Timothy Laurence. Captain Phillips, who grew up in Great Somerford, near Malmesbury, continues to direct the annual Gatcombe horse trials, which attracts visitors and competitors from all over the world. Zara Phillips, daughter of the Princess and Capt

Phillips, was awarded an OBE in the 2007 New Year's Honours List after being named BBC Sports Personality of the Year.

3: **Holy Cross Church, Avening** is considered one of the most important Norman churches in the Cotswolds, built by Queen Matilda, wife of William the Conqueror. Before meeting William, Matilda fell in love with a young lord called Brittic, who then held Avening Court. Her advances were spurned. After her marriage to

Holy Cross Church, Avening

William and his accession to the throne, she took her revenge. Matilda persuaded the King to have Brittic imprisoned at Worcester, where he died. In remorse, she had Avening Church built so that prayers could be said for his soul. Its consecration on September 14th 1080, when the royal couple gave a boar's head to the villagers, continues to be celebrated every other year on Pig Face Feast.

C: **Holy Cross Churchyard:** Film-maker Michael Powell (1905–1990), co-creator with Emeric Pressburger of such wartime British classics as *A Matter of Life and Death*, *Black Narcissus* and *The Life and Death of Colonel Blimp* is buried near the eastern boundary of the graveyard. Engraved on a simple headstone is the epitaph: "Film director and optimist". His grave is next to that of the actress Pamela Brown, who appeared in many of Powell and Pressburger's films and lived with Powell in the village for many years. She died in 1975.

18. BOX HILL

Distance:	4 miles
Time:	2 hours
Pub:	The Quarryman's Arms, Box Hill
Map:	OS: Explorer 156: Chippenham & Bradford-on-Avon
Star-rating:	** Moderate

This delightful route runs north east of Box village, along the By Brook valley, over the hill through which Isambard Kingdom Brunel's famous Box Tunnel passes and past Hazelbury Manor. It ends with glimpses of the Box Tunnel (Bath) entrance, and some of the beautiful houses in the village. Box straddles the A4 about 6 miles west of Chippenham. Park off the Market Place, Box.

Route:

Market Place is the second turning left after passing the Box Tunnel viewpoint, coming from the direction of Chippenham. Turn left out of the car park and on meeting the main road, continue straight on. Cross the road with care.

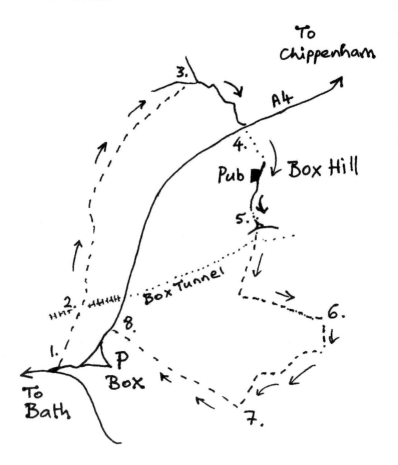

1. Take the first right signposted towards the library and bear diagonally right across the playing fields as indicated by the footpath sign. At the bottom far corner, join a track. At the end of this turn left onto a minor road.

2. Go under the railway bridge and continue along the road for about 200 yards. On a bend to the right, just before the river, take the footpath right past Peter Gabriel's Real World Studios housed in a converted mill. After crossing two footbridges, the path takes you alongside a field. Go over a stile on your left and follow the path across the field, keeping the river on your right. At the end of the field pass through the metal kissing gate, and continue with the river on your right through a second field to a stile. Keep a hedge on your right, soon to emerge onto a narrow lane via a stile.

3. Turn right. After about 50 yards go right again over a river bridge. Continue along the lane to start ascending **Box Hill (A)**. On coming level with Mill Platt (on your left), ignore the footpath striking off to your right. Turn right off the road as it bends left and climb some stone steps straight ahead, over a stile into a small field. Keeping a hedge and wall on the right, walk uphill until you reach a stone stile by the main road (A4). (To visit the picnic area and view point, turn right here.)

4. Cross the main road with care. Pick up the footpath opposite up some stone steps, bear left and pass a house on the right. Cross over a minor road, take the lane

View across the valley from Box Hill towards Colerne

GWR bench, Box Hill

ahead (Barnetts Hill) and continue uphill. Fork right near a telegraph pole. Soon you see the Quarryman's Arms (tel. 01225-743569) on your right. Continue past the pub along a narrow lane soon to fork left, past the common, to reach a well-placed pair of benches (again on your left) on Box Hill. There are good views towards Box and Middlehill and the northern outskirts of Bath from this spot.

5. Continue along the lane downhill passing to the right of a grass triangle. Cross the next road and enter woodland opposite via a gap. Take the left path of the three ahead through beech trees. Keep a boundary on your left. Before the path starts to descend take the left path to emerge from the wood. Take the path straight ahead (not the one on your right) and continue for about half a mile with a stone wall on your right.

6. Take the next footpath on the right across the middle of a field and soon turn right again onto a metalled lane. On reaching the complex of buildings at Hazelbury Manor, follow the track right and then left. At the next junction of tracks, follow the bridleway left downhill into woods.

7. Turn right at the next junction of paths and keep going all the way back into **Box (B)**.

8. On reaching the A4 main road again (via a junction with Bull's Lane) turn right, cross over to the pavement and go over the railway bridge to see the Bath portal of Brunel's famous **Box Tunnel (C)** from the viewing area over to your right. Otherwise go left and left again to return to the car park at Market Place.

Box Tunnel, Bath entrance

Notes:

A: **Box Hill:** Limestone quarries were worked here from the 8th century to create the distinctive honey-coloured Bath stone characteristic of the area. By the 19th century, the underground workings spread almost as far as Corsham. Parts of this complex of quarries were requisitioned by the War Department during World Wars I and II for storage, and a huge subterranean military base continued to operate here through the Cold War. For many years it was Whitehall's main nuclear bunker. The Quarryman's Arms, mentioned in numerous good pub guides, is especially popular amongst cavers, walkers, and the odd UFO watcher. Its walls are covered with quarrying memorabilia.

B: **Box** has several famous residents, past and present. The Rev. Wilbert V. Awdry (1911–1997), creator of the *Thomas the Tank Engine* books, spent most of his childhood in the village. He is said to have been inspired to write the stories by the sounds of the railway engines "talking to each other" as they came in and out of Box station just a few hundred yards from his father's vicarage. Ex-Genesis star Peter Gabriel created his Real World Studios in the village near the By Brook in the late 1980s, and the explorer David Hempleman Adams also lives in Box.

C: **Box Tunnel:** It took five years (1836–41), some 1200 navvies and 400 horses to build this 3,312-yard long tunnel for Brunel's Great Western Railway. Each navvy got through a ton of gunpowder and candles per week to blast their way through the stone, often in foul weather. More than 100 navvies died in accidents during the tunnel's construction. The elegant classic design of the Bath portal, framed by the magnificent backdrop of fields and woodland rising behind, creates a memorable sight. Corsham-based Rudloe Stoneworks has produced a Box Tunnel cast stone fireplace surround – there's one at the Quarryman's Arms, another at Chippenham railway station cafe.

19. FOXHAM

Distance:	4½ miles
Time:	2½ hours
Pubs:	Foxham Inn;
	Cross Keys, Bradenstoke
Map:	OS Explorer 156: Chippenham & Bradford-on-Avon
Star-rating:	*** More challenging

Spectacular views across the Vale of Dauntsey help to make this varied route from Bradenstoke to Foxham a real feast for the eyes. Mainly level or downhill, with a steep ascent on the return leg. You walk past RAF Lyneham airfield and near the remains of a medieval abbey, plundered on the orders of William Randolph Hearst, the American press baron and inspiration for Orson Welles' film classic "Citizen Kane". The old Wilts & Berks Canal, under restoration, also features along the route.

Route:

Park in the main road at Bradenstoke near Lyneham. From Malmesbury, take the B4040 to Swindon and take the first turning right to Little Somerford and Dauntsey. Follow the signs to Lyneham. Just before the sign indicating you are coming into Lyneham, turn right to

Bradenstoke. Try to park somewhere near the village shop – there are usually a few spaces available on the road. After parking, continue along this road past the Providence Chapel on your right and a No Through Road sign. After the last house on the right out of the village, take the footpath right and follow it around the edge of the field to a stile. Over to your left note the ivy-covered tower, once part of **Bradenstoke Priory (A)**.

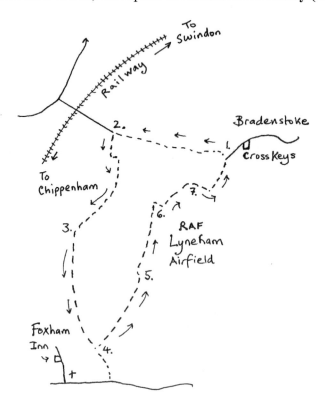

1. Follow the line of telegraph poles downhill then go over a footbridge. Go straight ahead through the next field down to a gate. Go through the gate. Keep a brook on your near left and pass through another gate onto a bridleway. Keep going until you emerge onto a road junction. Walk in the same direction for about 20 yards.

2. Go through the first of two gates on your left to continue between a post and rail fence and a hedge. Once in an open field walk diagonally left across it to

Wilts and Berks Canal near Foxham

reach a stile into the next field. Go straight on keeping to the left edge of the field. After entering the next field bear diagonally right across it towards a telegraph pole and a stile on your right. Turn left on reaching the other side of the field and follow the boundary to a stile in the corner. Cross the stile and soon a bridge on your right over the old Wilts and Berks Canal.

3. Turn left onto the towpath and follow the line of the canal for about a mile to reach a road running alongside **Foxham Locks (B)** and another bridge over the canal.

4. To visit the Foxham Inn (tel. 01249-740665) continue along the road to a T-junction. Turn right and walk along the verge, past the church and right again. You will soon see the pub on your right. Retrace your steps back to the canal bridge to continue the walk. If not visiting the pub turn left over the canal bridge just before some houses and follow the canal for about 20 yards before turning right through a gate to follow a track uphill.

5. After about half a mile's ascent turn right just before reaching a gate onto a sunken path between trees. Follow this path uphill again soon to meet a junction of tracks at a corner of the **RAF Lyneham (C)** perimeter

Climbing the hill above Foxham

Seconds after take-off:
a Hercules aircraft heads west from RAF Lyneham

fence. Go left here, keeping the perimeter fence on your right.

6. After Crash Gate 6 follow the path round to the right and past the RAF Saddle Club.

7. On reaching a new track bear right and follow it as it joins a road bending left back into Bradenstoke.

Notes:

A: **Bradenstoke Priory** was founded by Augustinian monks in 1142, and some of its ruins are still visible from the public rights of way – a tower and an arch, together with a perimeter wall and some outbuildings. Much of the structure and contents were dismantled in secrecy and taken to St Donat's Castle, near Llantwit Major, south Wales. This was done on behalf of William Randolph Hearst, the American press baron, and the real life Citizen Kane, immortalised by Orson Welles in the 1941 film. The dismantling of this important complex of medieval buildings caused a furore. Questions were asked in Parliament about the legitimacy of the sale to Hearst. St Donat's had been bought by Hearst in 1925, but the Bradenstoke treasures – the dismantled stones of the great tithe barn and a guest house – lay unused for years. Many pieces were shipped to the Hearst family mansion at San Simeon, California.

B: **Foxham Locks** served the old Wilts and Berks Canal, which is gradually being restored. Full restoration would reconnect the Thames (at Abingdon) with the Kennet and Avon Canal at Semington. At 60 miles, it is the longest canal restoration project in southern England.

C: **RAF Lyneham** is the home of the famous fleet of Hercules transport aircraft, nicknamed "Fat Alberts", serving the armed forces around the world wherever the UK has played a defence, humanitarian or peacekeeping role – from the Falklands and the Balkans, to Afghanistan and Iraq. Following a Ministry of Defence review, RAF Lyneham is due to close by 2012 with numerous functions and personnel dispersed to other MoD sites.

20. GATCOMBE PARK

Distance:	3 miles
Time:	$1^{3}/_{4}$ hours
Pubs:	The Bell Inn, Avening
Map:	OS Explorer 168: Stroud, Tetbury & Malmesbury
Star-rating:	** Moderate

This short walk across the high ground north of Avening offers sumptuous views towards Minchinhampton and Nailsworth. You go along the western edge of Gatcombe Park, home of the Princess Royal; and return to Avening via a hilltop golf course, and the boundary of another (one time) royal residence. There are two moderate inclines – one at the start and the other on the return leg. Avoid this walk during the Gatcombe Horse Trials (first week of August) when Steps Lane is temporarily closed. Avening lies about three miles north of Tetbury on the B4014, and is within about 15 minutes drive of Malmesbury. Park on the same side of the road as the Post Office and stores in Avening High Street, where the walk starts and ends.

Route:

Cross the road and walk all the way down Avening High Street passing the Bell Inn (tel. 01453-836422) on your left and follow the road as it bends round to the right. (To visit **Holy Cross Church (A)** take a turning on your left past the memorial hall and school.) Opposite the red Avening village sign turn right up Rectory Lane.

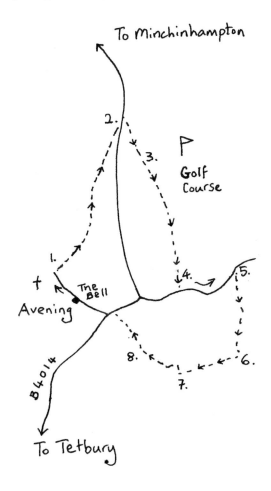

1. Take the next turning to the left, opposite a pair of telegraph poles, up a narrow tarmac path (Steps Lane), keeping an old stone wall on your right. This takes you through woods and then part of **Gatcombe Park (B)** cross-country course. Continue along the lane until you come to a road junction.

2. Turn left and after about 80 yards, cross the road with care and go over a stone stile in the wall. Go right, heading for another stone stile at the corner of a stone wall ahead. Go over this, and continue ahead keeping the field edge on your immediate right.

3. On reaching the far right corner of the field, cross over a third stone stile onto a golf course. The right of way is clearly signposted – follow the yellow tipped way-marked posts across the course. Aim for the right hand side of the clubhouse straight ahead, but before reaching it go to the right of a hedge then stay left of it to pass between the covered practice area and the clubhouse. Continue between a hedge (left) and a car park (right), and at the far left corner go through a gap in the hedge towards a low stone wall ahead. Cross a drive and bear left of a hedge ahead of you. Go straight on with the hedge on your right. Ignore the first gap in the hedge on your right (near a large cylinder) but pass through the second gap right and then turn left onto a track leading to a grassed area. Go straight on for

White Park cattle near Steps Lane, north of Avening

Leaving the golf course on the way to Nag's Head

about 30 yards. After passing a clump of trees on your right bear diagonally right onto a grassed corridor soon going downhill towards a tree-lined valley.

Exit the golf course via a wooden stile into a sloping field and a plantation of young trees. Follow the path downhill towards a "walk through" metal stile onto a road. On the other side of the valley ahead you may see part of the landscaped grounds of **Avening Court (C)**.

4. Once over the stile, turn left along the lane and through the hamlet of Nag's Head to reach a road junction before a red telephone box.

5. Turn right onto a well-defined path, go through a metal gate and bear right uphill, keeping trees and a small brook on your right. Pass through another metal gate, and proceed along the path with trees on each side. After the path becomes level, continue past a field on the right with a large stand of trees in the middle of it, which is marked on the OS map as Roundabout.

6. Go right over a stone stile just beyond the end of this field, and continue walking keeping a hedgerow and stone wall on your right and, beyond these, the stand of trees mentioned above. On reaching the end of this field, go over another stone stile and emerge onto a track.

7. Turn right here and, after about 150 yards, turn left over a stone stile and follow the path straight across a field. After going over another stile, the path soon bears right across a field. Exit the field via a wooden stile in the far right corner.

8. Turn right onto a lane going downhill. At the bottom of the lane, next to the Cross Inn, cross the road and walk back down Avening High Street.

Notes:

A: **Holy Cross Church, Avening and B: Gatcombe Park**. See the notes accompanying Walk 17 Avening.

B: **Avening Court** is mentioned in the Domesday Book. Legend has it that William the Conqueror (crowned William I) and Queen Matilda supervised the construction of Holy Cross Church while they were living at Avening Court.

21. BARBURY CASTLE

Distance:	$7\frac{1}{2}$ miles
Time:	$3\frac{1}{2}$ hours
Pubs:	The Crown Inn & The Bell, Broad Hinton
Map:	OS Explorer 157: Marlborough
Star-rating:	*** More challenging

This bracing trek brings panoramic views from the Ridgeway on the northern edge of the spectacular Wiltshire Downs, and an Iron Age hill fort. You then descend to the hamlet of Uffcott and the village of Broad Hinton. The path back up to your starting point offers views of the Broad Hinton White Horse. There's little shade or shelter along this route, so it's best avoided during very hot weather or when heavy rain is forecast. The walk starts and ends at the Hackpen Hill free car park on the Ridgeway, about 2 miles south east of Broad Hinton.

Route:

From Hackpen Hill car park, head east along the Ridgeway in the direction of a big clump of beech trees, with far reaching views away to your left.

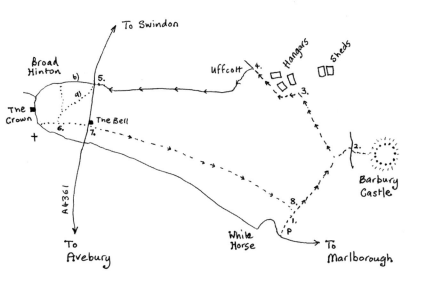

1. Once past the clump of beech trees, ignore the bridle-way signposted left to Broad Hinton and stay on the track up a gentle incline, soon to pass a second clump of trees. As the track becomes level, old aircraft hangars on the site of the former RAF Wroughton airfield can be seen in the valley on your left. The **Science Museum (A)** now occupies part of this complex. Continue ahead to reach a junction of tracks right by the foot of Barbury Down.

2. Turn right and then left through a gate onto Barbury Down. Proceed uphill along a clear path through the country park to **Barbury Castle (B)**. You can follow the

163

Walkers, Barbury Castle

path across the middle of the hill-fort, but for the best views north west towards the Cotswold Hills, and south across the downs towards Marlborough, take the circular path left that takes you along the outer ramparts all the way round and back to your starting point. Retrace your steps down the path you came up back to the Ridgeway, turning right at the gate and then left – as if returning to the Hackpen Hill car park. After about 300 yards, take the first right signposted By Way onto a track in the direction of some hangars and metal sheds ahead. Continue downhill on the track.

3. After about a mile stay on the track as it bends left and then shortly right. At the gated entrance, on your right, to the site containing three large old aircraft hangars you reach a junction of paths. Go straight on.

4. On reaching a road junction, go left to pass through Uffcott. Note the interesting thatched chalk wall on your left, once used to accommodate bee-hives. Continue along this quiet road for about a mile, past a duck pond on your right, an equestrian centre and another

The thatched chalk stone wall at Uffcott

pond on the left. On a clear day you should be able to see the Broad Hinton White Horse on your left.

5. At a crossroads, walk over the main road (A436) Swindon to Marlborough) with care, and continue ahead a few paces to reach a stile on the left into a field Here you have a choice – a) to follow the right of way through the fields into Broad Hinton or b) take an alternative route following roads and alleyways.

a) The stile into the field on your left, and another later on, may be difficult to cross. However if you do get over it, bear sharp right across the field to meet a pair of stiles separated by a farm track. Once over these, bear diagonally left to the far top corner of the field. Go through a wide gate and after about 40 yards, turn right over a stile in the hedge onto a tarmac path. Turn left and follow the footpath round to meet some metal bars. After passing the first set of bars, turn left onto a track that brings you to a road. Turn right along the road, which is Post Office Lane.

b) Go straight on past the stile, and take the first road left into Fortunes Field, a modern housing estate. Follow this road as it bends left. At the end of the cul-de-sac, take the footpath running right between two hedges. Cross over the next road, and turn left along the pavement leading to another footpath. Continue past a stile (left) to reach a set of metal bars. After passing the first set of bars, turn left onto a track that brings you to a road. Turn right along the road, which is Post Office Lane.

6. At a T-junction, turn right through Broad Hinton to reach The Crown Inn (tel. 01793-731302). If you wish to visit **Broad Hinton Church (C)** first, cross the road and turn left near the old well. Return to Post Office Lane, and walk the length of it to reach the main road (A4361) again.

7. Cross the road with care and take the signposted bridleway ahead, which runs back up to the Ridgeway from the right hand side of The Bell (tel. 01793-731934). Keep the hedgerow on your right and pass some farm buildings. On the hillside over to your right, you should soon be able to see the **Broad Hinton White Horse (D)**. When the hedgerow ends, keep going straight ahead on the track, broadly in the direction of the large clump of trees on the Ridgeway which is furthest to the right. Go through a metal gate and keep walking uphill to reach another metal gate. Once through this, continue until you reach a T-junction with the Ridgeway. Go through one more gate to reach the Ridgeway track, and turn right.

Broad Hinton White Horse near the Ridgeway

8. Retrace your steps to the car park at Hackpen Hill.

Notes:

A: Science Museum Swindon: More than 18,000 objects are stored here, from hovercrafts and a Lockheed Constellation airliner to examples of early computers and **MRI** scanners. For more information visit www.sciencemuseum.org.uk or phone 01793-846200.

B: Barbury Castle: Around this iron age hill fort the Battle of Beran Byrig was fought in 556AD as the Saxons' campaign to conquer the Romano-British pushed south. Lying within the Wessex Downs Area of Outstanding Natural Beauty, the fort and surrounding landscape became a country park in 1971 and was designated a Local Nature Reserve in 2004. In 1991, a racecourse was created nearby for point-to-point meetings.

C: St Peter ad Vincula: The church is one of only about 11 in England to be dedicated to this particular saint – the name means St Peter In Chains. A church has stood on this site since Saxon times, although the present building dates from the 13th century. The church contains some remarkable tombs and memorials – look out for the "handless" family of Sir Thomas Wroughton a 16th century Sheriff of Wiltshire. The Rev. Vere Awdry, vicar of Broad Hinton from 1891–95, had a son called Wilbert who also took the cloth but is best known as the author of the Thomas the Tank Engine stories. See the notes accompanying Walk 18 Box Hill for more on the Rev. Wilbert Awdry.

D: Broad Hinton White Horse: Sometimes known as the Hackpen Hill horse, this figure was carved to commemorate the coronation of Queen Victoria in 1837. Henry Eatwell, parish clerk for 40 years, and Robert Witt of the Crown Inn carried out the work. The

carving, measuring 90 foot square, has a near neighbou.
– the Broad Town White Horse, about three miles
north. Distinguished former residents of Broad Town
include the late poet and critic Geoffrey Grigson (1905-
1985), his wife Jane Grigson (1928–90) the cookery
writer, and the great architectural historian Sir Nikolaus
Pevsner (1902–83). For further information about the
Ridgeway, see the Walk 15 Silbury Hill notes.

22. EDGEWORTH

Distance:	8 miles
Time:	4 hours
Pub:	The Daneway Inn and The Bell, Sapperton
Map:	OS Explorer 168: Stroud, Tetbury & Malmesbury
Star-rating:	*** More challenging

A tremendous walk through a wooded river valley from Sapperton via Pinbury Park to Edgeworth, one of the most remote Cotswold villages. The return leg passes the old Thames and Severn Canal, and the Daneway Inn, a fine walkers' pub in a beautiful location. Parking is available near Sapperton Church or in the centre of the village. Sapperton lies about 13 miles north west of Malmesbury, off the A419 Cirencester-Stroud road.

Route:

From the road junction near Sapperton church, take the bridleway signposted just behind the phone box. Follow the path to enter woodland and soon emerge into a sloping grassy glade. Cut across the glade keeping to the higher ground, with the woods on your right.

171

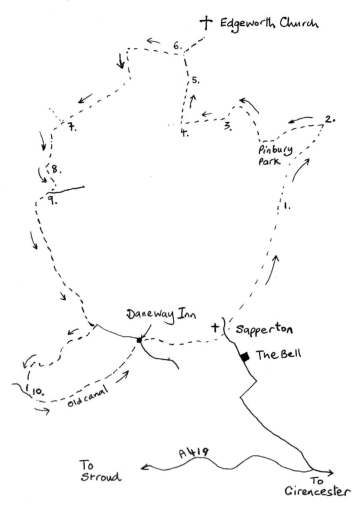

† Edgeworth Church

6.

5,

7.

2.

3.

4.

Pinbury
Park

8.

9.

1.

Daneway Inn

† Sapperton

The Bell

10.

old canal

A419

To
Stroud

To
Cirencester

1. Follow the track downhill through trees to pass through a wide wooden gate into the undulating landscape of **Pinbury Park (A)**. Continue straight across the field.

slightly to the right of the large house in the distance ahead. The path bends gently round to the right between two telegraph poles, following the contours of the hillside. Pass to the right of a large pond.

2. Turn left onto a tarmac drive and stay on it past the buildings on your right. Soon the route bends right and downhill to cross a stream via a wooden footbridge. Bear left to pass between two post and rail fences, and go through a wooden gate ahead into woodland. After about 500 yards of steady ascent on the track, go through a wide metal gate into a field.

3. Continue uphill keeping a metal fence on your right. At the corner of the field, go through another metal gate, and a third gate at the brow of the hill.

4. Turn right at this junction of paths, go through a wooden gate and continue straight ahead, keeping a stone wall on the right. Carry on in the same direction through this field and the next. Soon you see a sweep of parkland over to the right and Edgeworth Manor perched on the hillside ahead.

5. After passing through two wooden gates, walk downhill through parkland, keeping a metal fence on your left for about 100 yards. Aim for the house on the left in the group ahead of you, as the path descends more steeply.

Cattle near Sapperton

St Mary's Church, Edgeworth

On approaching the house, follow the path as it bends right to reach a gate. Pass through the gate to join a tarmac track, which takes you to **Edgeworth (A)** and its church. Retrace your steps back to the gate near houses.

6. Instead of taking the footpath left, back the way you came from Sapperton, take the path going right uphill to meet a track. Carry on in the same direction to meet a minor road. Turn left onto the road, then shortly right, opposite the entrance to some buildings.

7. Where the lane bends sharply to the right take the footpath left into a field. Go down the hill, keeping a metal fence on the left soon to join another path going left to right in front of you, just before a line of electricity poles. Turn left onto this path to go over a low wooden fence. Continue downhill to another stile at the far right bottom corner. Go over the stile and carry on downhill, over a tiny wooden footbridge and turn right to enter another field via a stile by a telegraph pole.

8. Bear left to continue downhill and stay close to the fence and hedge line on your left. Go through a gap in the hedge line and carry on for about 80 yards. Then turn right and aim for the metal gate high on the other side of the valley.

9. Go through this gate and turn right onto a lane. At a T junction cross the road, turn left and continue walking along this minor road for about half a mile, passing three footpath signs on the right. Go right at the fourth footpath sign (where a sign for Spring Bank House is attached to a tree). After about 20 yards go through the wooden gate on the left, behind which is a Gloucester shire Wildlife Trust sign. Stay on this path around the bottom of a hill on your left.

10. On reaching a T-junction of tracks turn left onto a wide path. After about 100 yards, go right over a stone bridge, then immediately left to follow the route of the former **Thames and Severn Canal (C)** through **Siccaridge**

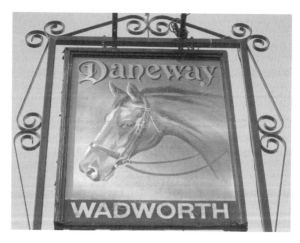

Daneway Inn sign

Wood Nature Reserve (D) for about three-quarters of a mile. You emerge onto a road by the Daneway Inn (tel. 01285-760297), originally built as three cottages to house workers constructing the waterway. Go over the road bridge, and pick up the path on the left marked **Wysis Way (E)**. Soon you pass the Daneway portal of the Sapperton Tunnel, and the path take you over the top of this into a field. Follow this path uphill to a kissing gate to return to Sapperton. The Bell (tel. 01285-760298) is on the road going uphill opposite the church.

Notes:

A: **Pinbury Park:** The manor was reputedly built on the site of the royal residence of Penda, the 7th century King of Mercia. After the Norman Conquest, the manor was given to the Abbess of Caen. In the 1890s, the Arts and Crafts architect Ernest Barnsley, his brother Sidney and their business partner Ernest Gimson moved in. Together they had a huge influence on the surrounding area, designing, renovating and furnishing houses – notably nearby Rodmarton Manor. Poet Laureate John Masefield lived at Pinbury Park from 1933–40.

B: **Edgeworth:** The manor was built in about 1700, although the church of St Mary next to it is of Saxon origin. Stunning views of the valley can be had from the end of the churchyard. The publisher, philanthropist and Labour peer Lord Hamlyn of Edgeworth (1926–2001) had a home in the village – one of four he owned in England and France. Tony Blair ennobled him in 1997 in recognition of his patronage of the arts and the underprivileged via his charitable trust, the Paul Hamlyn Foundation, valued in the early 1990s at £64 million.

C: **Thames and Severn Canal:** see the notes accompanying Walk 6 Sapperton Tunnel.

D: **Siccaridge Wood Nature Reserve:** Managed by the Gloucestershire Wildlife Trust, this magical area of ancient coppice woodland and wetlands provide habitats for numerous species including the common dormouse, water shrew, wagtail and dipper. Otters visit the River Frome which runs near the canal route.

E: **Wysis Way:** This 55-mile route was created to link Offa's Dyke with the source of the Thames near Coates, a few miles away from here, via the Forest of Dean and the Severn Vale.

23. BRINKWORTH

Distance:	4 miles
Time:	1¾ hours
Pubs:	The Three Crowns, and The Suffolk Arms, Brinkworth
Map:	OS Explorer 169: Cirencester & Swindon
Star-rating:	** Moderate

This route through the countryside around England's longest village offers fine views across the Vale of Dauntsey. You walk alongside, under and over the Swindon to Cardiff railway and back over Ramps Hill, south west of Somerford Common. Starts and finishes in Brinkworth, 5 miles east of Malmesbury on the B4042 Swindon road and on the 31 Andybus route.

Route:

From the recycling area and bus stop just beyond the Three Crowns (tel. 01666-510366) **Brinkworth (A)** go over the stile into a field and follow the left hand field edge round the back of the village hall to reach another stile round the next corner.

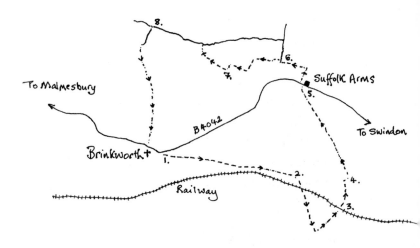

1. Go over the stile and go straight ahead past the rear boundary of a house. Carry on in the same direction downhill keeping a hedge on your left. Continue over a pair of stiles into the next field and head diagonally right across it downhill in the direction of the **railway line (B)**. Go over a stile at the bottom right corner, and turn left keeping the railway line on your right. Cross another two stiles, and the track beyond it. Continue in the same direction keeping parallel with the railway line. Go through a gap and straight across the field. In the far right corner, cross into the next field via a pair of stiles linked by a footbridge over a ditch. Turn left and aim for the metal gate in the middle of the gate ahead. Go through the gate and bear diagonally right across the field towards a wooden gate.

2. Go through the gate (or over the stile next to it) to pass under the railway. Bear left across the next field towards a gate (look out for two pill boxes behind you) and go through the gate. Turn right keeping a field edge, and soon a stream, on your right (Grittenham Brook) to the corner of the field. Don't go over the stile ahead. Instead, turn left uphill keeping a hedge and a barbed wire fence on your right. Turn left again at the next corner (ignore the gate on your right) soon to reach a gate at the top of the field.

Footpath under the railway east of Brinkworth

3. Once through the gate, turn left onto a bridge over the railway line onto a track. A few yards after the bridge, take the footpath (right) running parallel to the track towards farm buildings. Rejoin the track via a stile and on reaching the farmyard turn right.

4. After a few yards, turn left onto another track opposite the entrance to a large house. Keep going in the same direction all the way to the top of the hill. Just before the back gardens of some houses, turn right through a gate, and left to reach the main road (B4042) via another gate. (The Suffolk Arms (tel. 01666-510436) is a few yards to the right on the other side of the road.)

5. Turn left along the grass verge adjoining the main road, then cross the road to join Bellamys Lane opposite. Continue along the lane down the hill until you see a bridleway signed left just beyond a 30 mph sign. Turn left onto the bridleway and continue past the back of some houses, keeping a hedge on the left.

6. On reaching a road, cross over, turn right and soon go left to continue on the bridleway which soon bends round to the left towards a red brick-built house. Turn right by the house and follow the track downhill.

7. Ignore the first track bending left and continue downhill. After a house on the right, but before another on

your left, turn right through a parking area and go through a metal gate leading to a footbridge over a stream. After crossing over the stream, carry on in the same direction, keeping a hedge on your left and head towards a stile into the next field. Bear diagonally right across this into the next field and then go over a stile beside a wide wooden gate. Turn right – soon to emerge onto a lane. Turn left onto a grass verge and continue alongside the lane, sloping gently uphill, for about half a mile.

8. After passing Hulberts Green Farm, go through a metal gate on the left onto a bridleway. Keep a hedge on your left as you walk downhill. Ignore the first stile (left) but where the ground becomes level – about two thirds of the way down the field – cross the pair of stiles on the left. Bear right for 80 yards or so to cross a small fence set in a hedge, and then keep going with a hedge on your left down to a stile at the far left corner of the field. Keep going through this field and then into the next to begin your ascent of Ramps Hill. Go over a stile in a gap in the hedge to emerge near the top of the hill. Stay on the path around the right side of the hill, keeping a field boundary on your right, and the tower of Brinkworth church in your sights ahead. Follow the path downhill over a track and into a field. Continue straight and past the right side of the end house ahead

View south towards Brinkworth from Ramps Hill

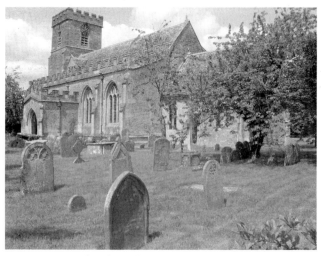

St Michael and All Angels, Brinkworth

to reach the main road (B4042) near the church. Turn left to return to the recycling area and bus stop.

Notes:

A: **Brinkworth** is England's longest village stretching 4¾ miles east to west and almost that distance north to south – from the hamlet of Braydon to Tockenham Wick. In 2006, new road signs were erected to mark Brinkworth's claim to fame. From the churchyard of St Michael and All Angels, on the western side of the Three Crowns, there are spectacular views over the Vale of Dauntsey, and the skyline towards Bristol and the Severn estuary. St Michael is said to be patron saint of the airborne, and is associated with all high places.

B: **The Swindon to Cardiff railway** running via Bristol Parkway (originally Bristol Patchway) is sometimes also known as the Badminton line. It strikes off Isambard Kingdom Brunel's original GWR (London to Bristol Temple Meads) mainline just west of Wootton Bassett passing south of Brinkworth, Little Somerford and Rodbourne and then north of Hullavington and Acton Turville.

24. NORTON & HULLAVINGTON

Distance:	6½ miles
Time:	3½ hours
Pubs:	Radnor Arms, Corston; Vine Tree, Norton; Star Inn, Hullavington
Map:	OS Explorer 168: Stroud, Malmesbury & Tetbury
Star-rating:	*** More challenging

Binoculars are recommended on this walk as you may spot deer, buzzards and other wildlife around the open countryside between Corston, Hullavington and Norton. Starts and finishes in Hullavington, about four miles south east of Malmesbury off the A429 Chippenham to Cirencester road. A number 92 bus runs between Malmesbury and Hullavington Monday to Saturday. If driving, park near the post office and stores off the main road (The Street) in Hullavington village.

Route:

With the post office and stores behind you, turn right along The Street, Hullavington, soon to pass the primary school on your left, and the cemetery on your right. On reaching a crossroads, go straight ahead on a No Through Road for 1/4 mile towards Court Farm soon to pass under a railway line (Swindon to Cardiff via Bristol Parkway, the old Badminton line). Continue under the railway bridge along the track for about another 400 yards, via a ford (or footbridge to the left). After about another half a mile enter a field at the end of the track.

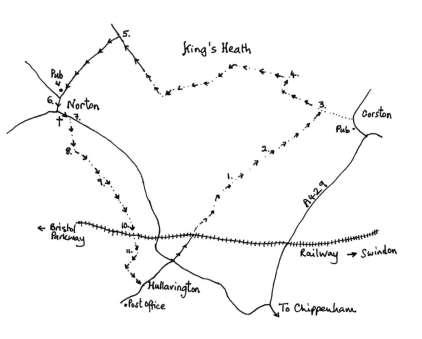

1. Go on in the same direction following the path straight across the field in front of you, alongside a row of oaks. Go through a gateway in the hedge. Continue along the

Railway bridge north east of Hullavington

left edge of the field to reach another gate by an oak tree.

2. Go through the gate, turn right and follow the path. Go through a gate and continue along the path keeping a hedge on your right. Go through a gate at the end of this field, with Gauze Brook on your left, then walk over a stone bridge to cross the brook. Follow the path up to a wooden gate onto Mill Lane,

Corston. (To visit the Radnor Arms (tel. 01666-823389) go right from here and then right again on reaching the main road (A429). Then return to this spot, continue along Mill Lane and follow the instructions from point 3 below.)

3. Turn left along Mill Lane and after West Park House enter parkland with woodland (West Park Wood) over to your left. Carry on up the hill, past a line of trees and a private drive on your right. Immediately after this drive, take the first footpath signposted to your right via a gate. Follow this path keeping the hedge on your right, to reach a lane (Common Road).

4. Turn left onto Common Road. Where the road bends right go straight ahead onto a track past Lower West Park Farm. The large tract of open flat land you see to your right and ahead is **Kings Heath (A)**. A few hundred yards past the farm, ignore the track on your right going across King's Heath. Carry straight on for about $^3/_4$ mile until you meet woodland straight ahead of you. Here, turn right along a track for about $^3/_4$ mile past farm buildings on the left.

5. At a road junction, turn left along the road or the grass verges to the village of Norton and the Vine Tree pub (tel. 01666-837654) on your right.

The Vine Tree, Norton

6. Follow the road as it bends left over the ford/footbridge and go left at the next T-junction. (To view **Norton Church (B)** turn right after a few paces into a No Through Road.) Continue along the road downhill and immediately after crossing the road bridge over the stream you will find a stile into a field on the right.

7. Climb over the stile, and then walk diagonally uphill to the opposite corner of the field. Here you will find a stile to the right of a gateway in the hedge.

8. Go over the stile and turn left following the left field edge. Go over the next stile and footbridge at the end of this field.

9. Go straight ahead through the next field, aiming for the middle of three ash trees ahead to join a track. Where the track bears round to the left, go straight ahead. Keep to the right of a hedge on your left. Cross a ditch and another stile and carry straight ahead, with the hedge still on your left. You may see the railway line (or hear a train) over to your right. Go over another stile and past the back of a large property **Bradfield Manor (C) and a yew hedge.**

10. Go through a gap to your left and turn immediately right before a stone wall downhill towards, and over, a gate and then through a tunnel under the railway. Go left downhill over a wooden footbridge and then left uphill past a sewage treatment works. Walk straight across the field to the left of a telegraph pole ahead of you. Aim for the next telegraph pole ahead, at the corner of a hedge and walk downhill a few paces, with the hedge on your left, to cross a small stream and a stile. Bear right towards a large ash tree, below cottages and another stile next to a gate.

11. Turn next right before reaching the cottages following their rear boundaries to an opening near a corner of the

field. Go left through the opening and then straight ahead into a road called Newtown, which then joins the main road through Hullavington. Turn right here to visit the Star Inn (tel. 01666-837535), and return to your car or the bus stop.

Notes:

A: **King's Heath** – see the notes accompanying Walk 2 Corston.

B: **All Saints, Norton:** "Humble with a presumptuous bell-turret" was Pevsner's verdict of this church, in a beautiful spot, next to the walled garden opposite Norton Manor.

C: **Bradfield Manor** is one of the few surviving great halls of the 15th century. According to the antiquarian writer John Aubrey, Bradfield was a distinct parish with its own chapel in medieval times. William Collingbourne, owner of the manor in the late 15th century was executed in 1485 for conspiring against Richard III and plotting to have Henry Tudor, the Earl of Richmond, installed on the Throne in his place. In November 2004, ex-Tory MP Neil Hamilton and his wife Christine bought Bradfield Manor.

25. BROKENBOROUGH

Distance:	7 miles
Pub:	Rose and Crown, Brokenborough
Time:	3 hours
Map:	OS Explorer 168: Stroud, Tetbury & Malmesbury
Star-rating:	** Moderate

A charming walk from Malmesbury to Brokenborough and beyond along the meandering Tetbury Avon, across farmland then back to the town past a good country pub. You pass the spot where two Tamworth pigs made a famous escape. An optional short cut takes you to the pub sooner and lops about three miles off the distance above.

Route:

From the Market Cross, Malmesbury, go along Birdcage Walk next to the newsagent's shop, then right into Gloucester Street. At the war memorial turn right down Gloucester Road to a mini-roundabout.

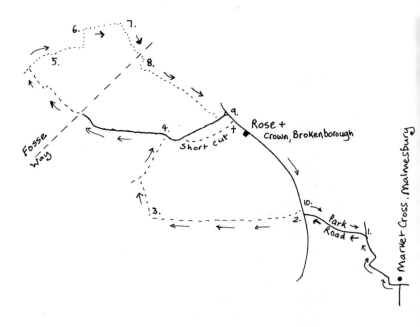

1. Turn left into Park Road. After about 300 yards, where the road bends left, turn right into a continuation of Park Road. On the site of the new housing development you now see on your left was the town's abattoir until the late 1990s. There began the tale of the **Tamworth Two (A)**. Keep going to reach a T-junction next to the **Tetbury Avon (B)**. Turn right over the river bridge (Back Bridge). After about 60 yards join the footpath signposted left into a field and pass a barn on your right.

Heading for Back Bridge along Park Road next to the Avon

2. Continue straight across the field to go through a gate next to a stile a few feet to the right of the river. After walking alongside the river a few yards, turn left through a gate into another field, keeping the river on your left and a hedge on your right soon to reach a farm gate. Go through the gate, and across the farmyard then turn right onto a bridleway.

3. Go straight on keeping a hedge and higher ground on your left. Go through a gate ahead. Bear left then follow the path right uphill. On reaching a T-junction, turn right.

4. At the next T-junction, turn left onto a lane to complete the full version of the walk (otherwise follow the *optional short cut after step 10 below). Carry on for about half a mile until you come to a track (the Fosse Way). Go left and almost immediately right over a stile in the hedge ahead into a field. Keep a post and rail fence on your left. Where the fence turns left, keep going straight on in the same direction and exit the field via a pair of stiles. Turn left onto a grass track, and almost immediately right on a path through a plantation of young trees. Follow the path on this diagonal line through the plantation as you cross over a wide grassed area soon to meet a stile ahead. Cross the stile soon to meet a drive. There are large stable buildings away to your left, and behind you a line of spectacular sweet chestnut trees. Here you have a choice:

a) To avoid any livestock in the field ahead, turn right onto the drive and at the bottom of the slope, turn left onto a grass walkway. Pass a stile on your left and soon go right to walk uphill between two post and rail fences to reach a T-junction of paths. Turn right soon to meet a drive.

b) If you prefer, you can go through the gate ahead and bear diagonally right downhill to pass through a gate. Turn left and almost immediately right to walk uphill between two post and rail fences soon to reach a T-junction of paths. Turn right onto a grassed track soon to reach a drive.

5. Turn right onto the drive and after about 50 yards, turn left onto another grassed track. Keep a hedge on your left and a post and rail fence on your right as you continue ahead. At a corner, go straight ahead through a gap in the hedge. Turn right onto a wide grassed area, with a hedge on the right and post and rail fencing on the left. Keep this fence on your left as it bends left soon to emerge in front of a stand of young trees just before a drive. Pass the trees and bear right onto the drive. Ignore the first turning right off the drive, but take the second one about 30 yards further on, to pass through a gap in the hedge.

6. Go through (or climb over) the wide metal gate in front of you into a long narrow field. Aim for the bottom left corner of the field, heading towards a gate near trees.

7. Go right at the corner, soon to reach the river Avon again. Keep it on your left and go over a stile next to it. Continue ahead keeping the river on your left. Go through a gate and across a track, the Fosse Way near a

Trish, Marion and dogs on the footbridge near Brokenborough

ford. Go over a stile and pass to the left of a metal gate into a field. Go straight on aiming for a gap in the tree line ahead. Go through the gap and then bear right towards a wide metal gate at the bottom of a hill.

8. After passing through the gate, turn immediately left and keep a barbed wire fence on your left as you walk uphill and turn left at a corner. After passing an area of scrub on your right the ground becomes level. About 100 yards after the scrub you reach the end of a grassy

Weathervane, St John the Baptist Church, Brokenborough

track coming from the right. Turn right onto this track to pass between two large cultivated areas soon to meet a hedge in front of you. Pass to the left of the hedge, and keep going in the same direction. At the other end of the hedge, go left along a track, keeping another hedge on the right. As the track starts to bend left, cross the stile on the right just beyond a wooden hand rail. Walk downhill through a field towards the right hand side of a house in the valley. Half way down the hill, bear right towards a footbridge over the Tetbury Avon into Brokenborough. Go up some steps after crossing the bridge to join a lane. Turn left.

9. Where the road forks, go past a yellow grit store and then right onto the main road through the village. Pass the church on your right. The Rose & Crown pub (tel 01666-822302) is about 250 yards further on to your right. Continue in the same direction after the pub soon to reach Back Bridge.

10. Turn left into Park Road and return to Malmesbury centre the way you came.

*Optional short cut:

Turn right at the T-junction, and on reaching the river, take the footbridge to the right of the river bridge. Follow the path up to the church and turn right at a T-junction. You will soon see the Rose & Crown on your right. Continue in the same direction down the road and turn left into Park Road after crossing Back Bridge. Return to Malmesbury the way you came.

Notes:

A: **The Tamworth Two:** Also known as Butch and Sundance, these two pigs saved their own bacon and became international celebrities in January 1998. They broke out of the abattoir, swam across the river opposite and spent nearly two weeks on the run, with television crews and cameras in hot pursuit. After their re-capture, and a spell at an animal sanctuary near Chippenham, the pair were re-homed at a rare breeds farm.

B: **Tetbury Avon:** Sometimes known as the Bristol Avon, the Wiltshire Avon has two sources, one near Tetbury the other near Sherston. The two branches meet east of Baskerville, Malmesbury. The river then winds its way to Avonmouth and the Bristol Channel via Great Somerford, Christian Malford, Chippenham, Reybridge, Melksham, Bradford-on-Avon and Bath.

Bibliography

Ashton Keynes
The Joyful Community – Benjamin Zablocki (Penguin Books, 1971)
Work on the Wild Side – Christopher Middleton (Daily Telegraph, 6/11/2004)

Avebury & Silbury Hill
A Zest for Life: The story of Alexander Keiller – Lynda J. Murray (Morven Books, 1999)

Avening & Gatcombe Park
Michael Powell – James Howard (Batsford Film Books, 1996)
The Buildings of England: Gloucestershire 1: The Cotswolds – David Verey and Alan Brooks (Penguin, 1999)

Box Hill
Isambard Kingdom Brunel – Adrian Vaughan (John Murray, 1991)
The Thomas the Tank Engine Man – Brian Sibley (Heinemann, 1995)

Cerney Wick, Sapperton Tunnel & Lacock
The Wilts and Berks Canal – L.J. Dalby (The Oakwood

Press, 2000)

The Thames & Severn Canal – Humphrey Household
(Alan Sutton and Gloucestershire County Library, 1987

Easton Grey

Almost A Fairy Story: A History of Easton Grey House –
Peter Saunders

Edgeworth

The Cotswold Village Trail – Nigel Bailey (Reardon
Publishing, 1998)

Foxham, Norton & Hullavington

The Chief: The Life of William Randolph Hearst – David
Nasaw (Gibson Square Books, London, 2002)

The Last Country Houses – Clive Aslet (New Haven, Yale
UP, 1982)

Wiltshire Airfields in the Second World War – David
Berryman (Countryside Books, 2002)

Lea

The Naked Gardeners – Ian and Barbara Pollard
(Papadakis, 2006)

The Malmesbury Branch – Mike Fenton (Wild Swan
Publications, 1990)

Ecko's of Cowbridge – Bob Browning (Cowbridge
Publishing, 2005)

Luckington
The Secret Servant: The Life of Sir Stewart Menzies: Churchill's Spymaster – Anthony Cave Brown (Michael Joseph, 1988)

Shipton Moyne
Shrinking fortune forces owner to sell ancient estate – (The Times, 24 October 1996).
Selkirk's Island – Diana Souhami (Phoenix, 2002)

Westonbirt
Highgrove: Portrait of an Estate – HRH the Prince of Wales and Charles Clover (Phoenix Illustrated, 1993)